THE SHARPER INVESTOR

THE
SHARPER
INVESTOR

THE WINNING FORMULA THAT
BOOSTS YOUR RETURNS

RICHARD
THALHEIMER

LIONCREST
PUBLISHING

THE SHARPER INVESTOR
The Winning Formula That Boosts Your Returns

ISBN   978-1-5445-2555-6   *Hardcover*
       978-1-5445-2554-9   *Paperback*
       978-1-5445-2553-2   *Ebook*
       978-1-5445-2670-6   *Audiobook*

CONTENTS

ABOUT RICHARD THALHEIMER AND THE SHARPER IMAGE

1977: THE BIRTH OF THE SHARPER IMAGE

In 1977, Richard turned $500 into an unforgettable retail empire by selling what he wanted to buy, which didn't yet exist. "America's Gadget Guy" didn't just ride market trends; he created them. The first catalog, mailed in 1979, featured the first cordless phone, answering machine, and car radar detector. Some people say that the "yuppie guys of the 1980s didn't have their own catalog until Richard gave them one."

1983: RICHARD APPEARS ON PRIME TIME TELEVISION PROGRAMS

Joan Rivers, Merv Griffin, Oprah, *60 Minutes,* and many more national television and newspaper outlets featured Richard as a special guest. He was instantly famous and heralded for his success. *The New Yorker* described him as the "very model of a major entrepreneur: tanned and muscular, deliberate and tenacious, and infallibly gifted at curating ridiculously niche gadgets."

1985: HOLLYWOOD CELEBRITIES FEATURED IN THE SHARPER IMAGE CATALOG & STORES

The Sharper Image catalog became a cultural icon and bragging rights for Hollywood's celebrities, many of whom were featured in the catalog before they were known. Raving movie fans have spotted The Sharper Image catalog or stores in *The Firm* featuring Tom Cruise, *When Harry Met Sally*, *Snow Dogs* with Cuba Gooding Jr., and *Sex In the City*. Many consumers remember The Sharper Image credit card used in *A View to Kill* with James Bond.

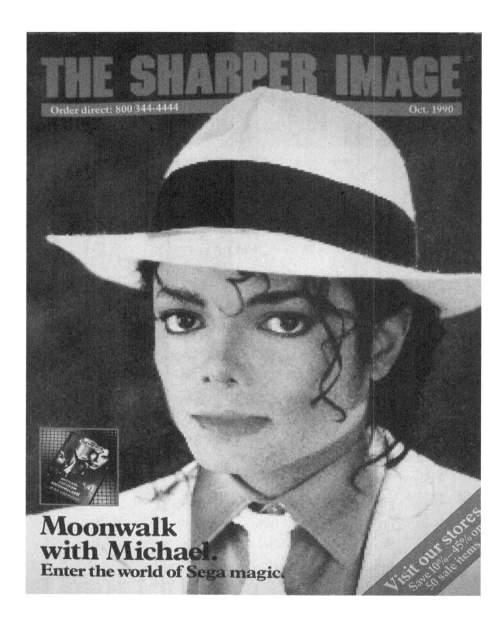

1987: NASDAQ LISTS THE SHARPER IMAGE AS SHRP

The Sharper Image IPO'd in 1987 with raving fans, and national publicity focused on Richard's extraordinary entrepreneurial creation. In the 1980s stock boom, flashy gadgets, and conspicuous consumption were in. "Having the most toys" was the mantra of the new decade. Richard found a way into the hearts of consumers who wanted something new.

1991: SHARPER IMAGE DESIGN BRAND LAUNCHES

An exclusive and secret incubator for "Sharper Image Design" labeled products launched in 1991 in Novato, California. Later dubbed a "Xerox Park for Gadgetry," this highly successful product design lab started with just a few engineers and designers. By the mid-nineties, two dozen employees were responsible for over 300 patents and 100 new products...from the useful to the exotic.

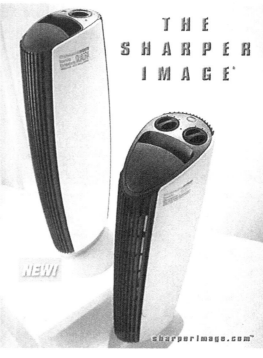

1996: STEVE JOBS & RICHARD CREATE A NEW E-COMMERCE EXPERIENCE

Wired Magazine wrote that the revolutionary partnership between Richard and Steve Jobs pioneered modern-day e-commerce. Jobs' innovations and Thalheimer's vision changed the retail sector forever by unveiling state-of-the-art digital display options and algorithms for SharperImage.com at Internet World Expo in 1996. When the internet was in its infancy, industry trades quoted Richard suggesting a future link of phones and websites (this was way before e-commerce options were available online) he termed "electronic stores." Yet again, Richard's prescient ability proved to be true.

2003: SHARPER IMAGE PEAKS WITH 200 STORES & 4,000 EMPLOYEES

With Richard at the helm in 1977, an initial investment of $500 worth of copy paper, and a $69 watch, it dramatically grew into a company with $760 million dollars in sales by 2003. In 1981, the first Sharper Image store opened in San Francisco, ushering in a new era of experiential retail that was uniquely immersive. The stores had a distinctive aspirational modern decor devised so that shoppers could, as Richard put it, "touch, feel, and play" with the merchandise.

2006: RICHARD LEAVES THE SHARPER IMAGE AND SELLS REMAINING SHARES

Three decades later in April of 2005, a private equity fund from New York City announced they had bought 12 percent of the company's public stock in open market purchases and were given board representation. Richard and these new board directors did not get along, so he left the management, though still the largest shareholder. In May 2007, he sold his remaining shares and began to pursue his passion for stock market investing full-time.

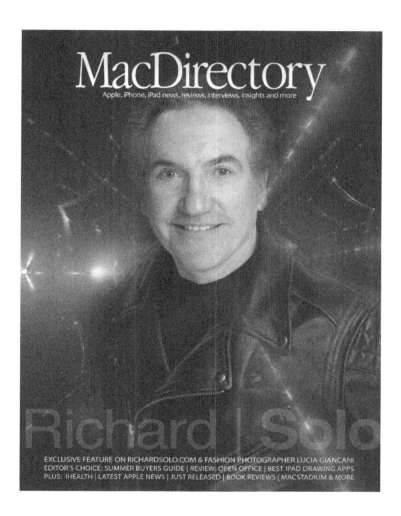

2019: YOUTUBE CHANNEL LAUNCHES— THE LEGEND OF THE SHARPER IMAGE

Over 300 videos can be seen online, such as nostalgic commercials, prime time TV appearances, interviews, and internal product updates that bring back feel-good memories for customers and employees. Curious viewers can even see behind-the-scenes business meetings that demonstrate Richard's intuitive and inspiring leadership skills in action.

6B

2020: BEST-SELLING BOOK, SHARPER IMAGE SUCCESS, HITS #1 ON AMAZON

Within a week of its launch, Richard's new book, Sharper Image Success: Business Lessons from America's Gadget Guy, received #1 Best Seller status in five categories on Amazon. In this best-selling book, he teaches that originality and mutually beneficial relationships are essential attributes of success. He shares his techniques for connecting with others in negotiation and collaboration. He writes about what he learned in life and his career: how to work with people, how to negotiate, how to sell, and how to make money.

My father, Alan Thalheimer, started teaching me about investing in stocks and options 40 years ago, and we have talked about it a lot. Without his help and advice, I would never have gotten to where I am today and achieved these terrific results. This book is dedicated to you, Dad!

ACKNOWLEDGMENTS

LILY THALHEIMER

I'd like to thank and acknowledge Lily Thalheimer, my daughter. We have worked together, and she has helped me grow our private fund since 2018.

It has been gratifying for me to see her do so well, and I've learned so much from her during this process. She has introduced me to some excellent stock choices that were not apparent until she brought them to my attention. Having previously led the product team at a design and consulting firm, Lily has the advantage of being super smart, understanding consumer-driven behaviors, and analyzing e-commerce, D2C, and tech companies from firsthand experience.

She has also helped me refine the techniques we discuss here. She is a sharp investor and achieved a 260% return in 2020. So, thank you, Lily, for helping me be a better trader and sharing your ideas and thoughts about stocks, the market, and trading.

You have been a great influence on me and made me a Sharper Investor!

XAVIER ESTRADA

Xavier Estrada, of Xavier Estrada Design, is the tal-

ented Chief of Brand Design, the driving force in my creative endeavors.

Xavier has over two decades of experience in the design field, specializing in UX/App Design, web marketing design, packaging, corporate branding, and photoshoot art production. In short, he brings strategic creativity to my brand identity and design. And, he does a great job on the covers of my books!

We share similar creative aspirations, tastes, and a passion for excellence. He's the right kind of creative genius to satisfy any visionary's aesthetic.

Xavier, you are a pioneer. Thank you for your friendship, your family-focused good nature, and your fantastic work. Your talent helped make The Sharper Image brand iconic and has impacted the major brand advertising trends we see today.

I'm delighted we have moved into the financial industry to help our readers—some new and some of our customers from The Sharper Image days—grow their personal wealth and empower their lives.

This is excellent work we are doing. Your rich creative mind reflects my imagination.

Thank you!

MEREDITH MEDLAND SASSEEN

I'd like to acknowledge my marketer, agent, writing consultant, and friend, Meredith Medland Sasseen.

Meredith has an incredible ability to listen to my ideas, desires, and dreams and make them happen. I'm

an entrepreneur with more than four decades of experience. I know how unique and valuable it is to partner with talented individuals who support the vision of another leader and help it come to life.

I dream bigger dreams when self-directed, action-oriented leaders back me up. Over the years, a dozen or so people have deeply listened to me, demonstrated an understanding of how I like to work, moved with the rhythm of the conversations I enjoy, and learned to communicate the details that are important to me. Meanwhile, they make decisions on their own that continually move the project forward. Some of those people can even see a vision for me that I have only caught a slight glimpse of for myself.

Meredith is one of those people. One of the things I appreciate most about Meredith is her ability to wear so many different hats and wear them well. She always keeps outcomes in mind but collaborates with fluidity and flexibility. It is rare to find someone who can vision, write, edit, and market.

This is our second book together; on both occasions, Meredith has supported me in expanding my ideas, putting potent words to them, and helping me get clear on my thoughts.

Meredith, thank you for investing your energy in our projects. I also want to acknowledge your trust in The Sharper Investor Winning Formula. I'm delighted it has worked for you, and I trust your wealth will continue to expand in all areas of your life. Thank you for supporting our community of readers.

With much gratitude,
Richard

FOREWORD

by Meredith Medland Sasseen

Richard hired me in 1999 as the Director of the Internet Division for The Sharper Image. Twenty years later, we reconnected at a company reunion and embarked on a new project together.

We gathered video content to create The Legend of Sharper Image YouTube Channel. Next, we began weekly interview-style phone sessions for his soon-to-be-published, #1 Best-Selling book, Sharper Image Success: Business Lessons from America's Gadget Guy.

These inspiring interactions were frequently punctuated by Richard's news of the latest stock market movements, Tesla trends, and the overall joys of his investing success. His enthusiasm for trading was pleasurably intoxicating.

I quickly realized that to really connect with Richard and write his book, my knowledge of the stock market would require a new level of depth.

Little did I know, this immersion would become a game-changer in my financial life. The more educated I became, the more Richard shared his investing strategies. His returns were extraordinary compared to other well-known hedge fund managers in the news. I was more and more impressed by his trading rules and results. His returns were unbelievable.

Money is transformative by nature. It brings up issues for all of us. That's where the magic begins. Chances are since you are about to read this book, you've already crossed the bridge into a new territory of economic transformation in your life. Now, you want more.

After several months of weekly engagements with Richard, I did too. My husband and I had often amused ourselves over morning coffee by imagining what it would be like to have Richard trading on our behalf. We thought, if he could make such fabulous returns with his own money, he could surely boost our return in contrast to my broker.

The broker had been working with my inherited money; the hometown ties and his long-time relation-ship with my father were strong. After I received the inherited money, I let it sit and never touched it. Too many emotions to confront.

I finally asked for help, and Richard immediately responded with generosity. Shortly after, I took his advice, sold all the positions, and wired the balance to my new online trading account with E*TRADE.

A wave of grief passed, and now it felt like the money was really mine. It was riveting yet terrifying. With an exact amount of total dollars to begin, I had the power to lose all the money I inherited and was also now empowered to boost my returns. I was determined to beat my broker.

Richard was incredibly patient and empowering as he began to teach me his formula. First, he showed me how the companies I cared about and how my prior life experience would inform my investing.

He walked me through the difference between investing the same amount of money in stocks versus options using simple mathematical equations. Then, he taught me how to mitigate risk as long as I was willing to make a long-term investment. I was so surprised, and I loved the formula. It was simple and easy to understand.

Richard's suggestions were consistent; even when I asked the same questions differently, his answers followed his formula every time. Three keys: buy long-dated calls, sell weekly puts, and choose companies I liked and knew something about.

His formula worked—every time. My account balance grew rapidly.

But then, after some extraordinary gains, I decided to move outside the formula with my newfound freedom and knowledge. That's when I experienced my first significant loss. It scared me, and I quickly recalibrated, humbly, as the beginner I was, and began using the formula to regain the loss. I learned my lesson, and my returns improved.

Then, the crash of March 2020 happened. I froze and became more conservative in my trading. Richard suggested that I slowly nibble in, just buying a little bit at a time. He said he had experienced things like this before, and even he had to nudge himself a little to continue trading. But he did. Why? Because that was his formula. He followed his own rules.

His emotional steadfastness and perseverance were incredible to witness. He was either brilliant or crazy. Which would it be?

In my mind, I questioned him and thought, how can you nibble in when the market is crashing? I stopped initiating new positions while he confidently nibbled in and bought long-dated calls.

Months and months went by, and my account balance stayed almost the same. Richard's grew. A lot. I watched and listened as he made trades; just like the years prior, his portfolio grew at an extraordinary rate, going way beyond the performance of many celebrity hedge fund managers.

As the market started to recover, he began selling weekly puts again. He continued to amaze me with his adherence to his simple formula. He increased his

E*TRADE portfolio from $50 million dollars immediately following the crash and finished the year at $200 million—a 400% return.

Fortunately, the market has just about recovered from that crash. And, I've begun trading again. (Using just the formula, of course.) And, Richard, well, he is still doing the same thing he has always been doing, rarely veering from his formula while his returns just keep on increasing. He is extremely successful, with higher returns than some of the hedge fund managers who make the front page headlines in the news.

So, what did we do next together? We wrote this book.

The formula, now called *The Sharper Investor Winning Formula*, is now available to you too. I hope you enjoy it. Just remember: stick to the formula, stay steady, and have fun!

Happy trading,

Meredith

Meredith Medland Sasseen

P.S. Richard regularly shares his trading and investing thoughts at *TheSharperInvestor.com*. Be sure to sign up to receive his email notifications, so you don't miss his insights and stock picks!

DISCLOSURE

Because we live in a litigious society, you notice every investment-related website has a legal disclosure designed to protect it from lawsuits. It is to remind you that past performance is not indicative of future results and that investing has a risk of loss of principal.

Let me disclose that I am not a registered money manager and that there is substantial risk in investing, and I am not responsible for you losing money. Furthermore, you should consult a professional money manager.

That sounds depressing, doesn't it? However, that is how disclosures are written—to paint the most dire scenario possible and to make you realize that a substantial loss could occur; and if it does, please do not consider me responsible for any of it! You are responsible for your decision-making.

There—I said it. Do not sue me if you lose money. It is not my responsibility, and I am making you aware of that fact.

Don't you love attorneys? They are responsible for how we got to this place. Since I am an attorney, I guess I am allowed to say that.

So...this section is the legal disclaimer: I am not responsible for anything, I am not holding myself out to be an expert on anything, and whatever happens to you is not my fault. And past performance is not an indication of future results. Got it?

I'm sorry that this disclaimer needs to be included in this book. However, that is the system we have nowadays. But that is what it is—a legal disclaimer!

Happy investing and best of luck!

Richard

INTRODUCTION

What is *The Sharper Investor?*

The Sharper Investor inspires you to use techniques that help you keep your losses to a minimum, maximize your returns, and do it in an intelligent way that makes sense. We can look at *The Sharper Investor* as a measurement of results, and the result we are looking for is a positive return of 30–50% a year on your investment portfolio. That may seem high, but it is attainable. I have done better than that most years. You can too!

We're not just counting on chance or luck to help us. We're exercising insight, analytical ability, and common sense to make the result come out the way we want.

This book is not intended to replace all the many investing books on the market. There are thousands of investing books. I don't pretend that I'm going to cover everything or that I'm even going to compete with them. We're not going to talk about evaluating financial statements. We're not going to use complicated ratios. We're not going to assess performance charts, and we're not going to predict market movements. I'll leave it to all the other excellent books available to teach you those other things. But we don't need them anyway.

All we need to do is pick the right stocks, buy call options, and sell put options. Very simple!

It's a very basic strategy, but it works. And that is the best part of it! You don't need to learn a lot of complicated stuff. Those things may be fun to learn about, but they are not used in my approach. If you follow the guidelines explained in these chapters, you will have an excellent opportunity to achieve extraordinary returns.

THE FORMULA THAT GETS RESULTS

This winning formula has been developed over 20 years of studying, investing, trial and error, and learning. It seems to be working well, and I'm excited to share it with you!

I understand some traders have more sophisticated tools and formulas. However, they have not produced higher returns than those I've experienced the past four years, averaging 110% a year—and 2020 was exceptional, with a 261% return. So while my formula can be criticized as too simple or not sophisticated enough, it's difficult to argue with the results!

The formula has three parts: We're going to choose the right stocks. We're going to sell put options that are a week or two out. We're going to buy call options that are two years out. There is a lot of detail and nuance for us to discuss, and combined with our winning three-part formula, you can get great returns.

As you will see, the formula is not complicated. It works for the new investor or the experienced investor. I must emphasize that each of these three parts must be done well. That's where I come in; this book will help guide you to use the formula in a smart and strategic way.

WILL YOU MAKE 50 PERCENT A YEAR?

I am not exaggerating when I say you can expect to make 30–50% per year. Anything more than 20 percent is considered superb, so going for 50 percent is quite a lofty goal. However, you can do it.

As a fun exercise, it is worth looking at the compounding at these rates.

- If you start with $100,000 and make 50% the first year, you will have $150,000. If you happened to make 50% the second year, you would have $225,000. If you made 50% the third year, you would then have $337,000.

- In the fourth year, if you made 50% again, you would have $505,500. In the fifth year, if you made 50%, you would add $252,750, for a total of $758,250.

- If you made 50% again, you would now be at $1,137,375.

By the end of the sixth year, that is more than a million dollars, starting with just $100,000!

This is entirely possible, using the simple but effective formula that we talk about in this book.

This strategy has produced an average return for me of over 100% a year for the last four years. One year was 92%, another was 96%, one was −10%. That was a bad year!

Then, 2020 was the best year, with a 261% return.

When I put those four years together, that's over 110% average return per year. Of course, it might not continue. It probably is unrealistic to expect, for me at least, that after four years of over 100% returns, the following year will be another year of over 100% returns. But 50% would be a great result also, and even 30% would be stellar.

Some people might wonder if this is similar to gambling or sports betting, in the sense that you're putting your bet out, you're going to win or lose, and you're doing it on your computer or iPhone. I disagree because we use our talent, intelligence, knowledge, and common sense to make bets that have a solid reason to succeed. It is not luck, and it is not chance.

CAN WE DO BETTER THAN SUCCESSFUL HEDGE FUND MANAGERS?

As a Sharper Investor, you can get better investment returns than the average hedge fund manager, and not just a little better, but a lot better. Most investment managers compare themselves to the broad averages, particularly The Dow Jones Industrial Average, the S&P 500, or the Nasdaq. Those are big indexes, which are generally considered to be the benchmarks. Like a hedge fund, if you can beat the benchmarks, that's terrific. Over the last 50 years, the stock market, in general, has risen on average, 10 percent a year. It has its up years and its down years, but these indexes have averaged about 10 percent up a year over the years.

As you probably know, most fund managers and money market managers strive to get returns of 12–18% a year, or in a rare case, 20% a year. Warren Buffett, perhaps the most famous investor of all time, managed to make a 17% average annual return for 20 years of investing. According to CNBC, "Berkshire Hathaway has posted average annual returns of 17.1% since 1985, well ahead of the broader stock market's 10.5%, including dividends. If you'd invested $10,000 in Berkshire Hathaway at the start of 1985, you'd now have $2.4 million; the same principle in the S&P 500 would now be worth about $227,000."[1]

That result by Buffet is considered truly stellar. The best hedge fund managers in the country don't usually reach 30%. I read an article in January 2021 listing ten of the top US hedge fund managers for 2020. The number one fund in the article had earned a return of about 67%. Then, it dropped down to a 50% gain for the second-best fund, the third position was a 40% fund return, and the fourth position was a 37% fund return. This shows that if we can make 30–50% a year, we're doing fabulous compared to even the best hedge funds. And bear in mind, 2020 was somewhat atypical with especially high returns.

It's a mixed bag when you look at the world of hedge fund stars. Some fund managers have done very well, some years making 30–50% returns, but then other years, they do negative 30–40% returns. Few managers can consistently turn out great positive results year after year.

---

1   Frank Thomas. "Warren Buffett Has Kept the Same Investing Philosophy for Decades, Early Interview Shows," *CNBC*, Sept. 22, 2019, www.cnbc.com/2019/09/22/warren-buffetts-investing-advice-consistent-over-past-35-years.html.

And when you look at the hedge fund industry as a whole, their results are mediocre. In 2020, a really good year, the industry average return was 11.8%, according to data group HFR.[2]

This observation that most managers with great results follow up the following year with some poor results may someday apply to *The Sharper Investor*, though I certainly hope not! The past four years have seen outstanding results.

NOTHING FANCY, BUT IT CAN PRODUCE RETURNS OF AS MUCH AS 30% OR MORE

There's nothing fancy here. I know a guy who is a very experienced and successful trader, and we were talking last year, and he was marveling at how good a return *The Sharper Investor* has been producing in The Sharper Fund. And he said, "You must have a really fancy trading room, with ten screens going on at one time, as you should have," and I said, "No, actually, I do it mostly on my iPhone or my MacBook." He laughed and said, "Oh, you've got to be kidding me. That's not possible." I replied, "Well,

---

2   Robin Wigglesworth and Laurence Fletcher. "A Hedge Fund Revival? Industry Hopes a Dismal Decade Is Over," *Financial Times*, August 20, 2021, www.ft.com/content/c87d52b2-d54e-4dae-9b50-98ca1e6c1d4c.

yes, it is." We're using a very simple approach to trading. And, that's the thing I like about it. It's not complicated, you can learn it easily, and we don't need ten screens.

Everything you will be working with is online, and very affordable. An E*TRADE account is free, and stock trading is free. Options trading still has a small commission, so it is not free, but it doesn't matter since the commission is so low. We are looking for returns that easily cover the cost of trading. In effect, the entire platform is just about free. I'll cover how to set up an account and get started later in Chapter 2.

For now, you need a source of investing ideas so that you can find your favorite stocks to invest in. You might want to use a subscription service online to access some sources of information, like *Action Alerts PLUS*, which I highly recommend (though I get no compensation for recommending it). Still, you can also get a wealth of financial news for free on websites like CNBC.com or MarketWatch. com. You can also get some of those ideas by subscribing to my email list at TheSharperInvestor.com, because I talk about my favorite stocks in my occasional blogs, and it is free. And you will have favorite companies that you use every day, like Chipotle, Amazon, Apple, and others that are public stocks.

By the way, this can all be done on your phone, tablet, or computer. And it is very entertaining. When you think about all the time that people put into their Facebook viewing time, or their Instagram viewing time, when you could be trading on E*TRADE and making money, I think you might agree it's a better use of time, and just as much fun, to trade and make money on E*TRADE. I spend no time on Facebook or Instagram, but I spend hours a day reading financial news and making trades online.

I realize that my system is open to criticism. Professional or experienced traders might think it too simple or even naive. It is always easy to criticize. However, the last four years have been consistent, and the results speak for themselves. The system we're working on together here enables us to get those types of returns.

MY STOCK TRADING BACKGROUND

Why should you take my advice? I started with trading stocks and options in college. And that was a long time ago, since I graduated from Yale in 1970. I definitely remember making some money and losing some money. And back then, losing some money was a big deal because it meant a lot more to me then as a percentage of my net worth. I tried many things over the years.

My business career was that of The Sharper Image catalog and retail store, which I founded in 1977. Throughout my time at The Sharper Image, I learned how to run a successful company, how to generate meaningful growth, how to manage risk, and above all, how to make money. I was so busy with building The Sharper Image that I really didn't have the time to devote to stock trading until I left The Sharper Image in 2006. However, my experience talking to analysts for 20 years as the CEO of The Sharper Image has given me great insight into how Wall Street analysts think, and consequently, when and why investors should confidently follow their judgments.

Since then, I have worked hard to refine my investing approach. I especially learned from the Najarian brothers, whose advice changed my investing career. They're big proponents of the proposition that you're better off buying call options than buying the actual stocks directly. They spend hours at their seminars explaining and proving that call options make a much better return for you than buying stocks. That's what I've been doing ever since I met them, and it's really paid off in boosting my overall returns. I'm now consistently earning average returns of 50–100% per year.

Using what I learned from them and combining that with my own experience, I'm getting excellent returns. In 2015, I launched my private fund, The Sharper Fund, known for its aggressive formula, including put options, long-dated call options, and holding stock positions in publicly listed US-based companies.

I've narrowed the for-
mula for success down to
a select choice of options,
which you'll hear over
and over from me. Basi-
cally, it's first and most
importantly choosing the
right stocks, buying long-
dated call options that
are two years out, and
selling put options that
are a week or two from

expiration. I frequently post blog entries on *TheSharperIn-
vestor.com*. This way, readers like you get a sense of some
of the real-time trades I make, understand why I choose
the companies I do, and see the sources I use to educate
myself. If you'd like to subscribe, go to *TheSharperInvestor.
com/book* and join our community.

CHAPTER 1

WHO IS A SHARPER INVESTOR?

THE SATISFACTION OF TRADING OPTIONS—AND DOING IT PROFITABLY

Investing in the market is an incredible adventure, which is extremely satisfying when you do it successfully.

I don't think there is anything more fun or exciting for me than to wake up when the stock market opens at 6:30 a.m. in California, light up the screen on my computer by the bed, and watch the opening market action. Some mornings it is up, and sometimes it is up a lot, and that is a great wake-up—better than a strong coffee! Other mornings it opens down, maybe even down sharply, and while that is discouraging, it is the most suitable time to place the type of orders we use.

Often, the market moves a lot each day, both up and down, from the opening; I understand that, and look at the morning hour opening numbers to realize it might change a lot by the end of the day. There have been many days when the market changed dramatically, for the better, or for the worse, from where it opened in the morning. Even though I know the opening market numbers will probably change, I still get excited and look with anticipation at my portfolio when the market opens. On the weekends, when the market is closed, I get bored! The weekdays are much more exciting!

THE SHARPER INVESTOR

What makes up the character of a *Sharper Investor*, who can get 30–50% a year return on their portfolio? It is a combination of talent, intellect, knowledge, common sense, and a bias toward action.

Talent means that you have some affinity, some understanding, of the ebbs and flows of the stock market. My skill with stocks results from being the CEO and creative leader of The Sharper Image stores and catalog. I started in 1977 with one product and one magazine advertisement. I had found a particular runner's watch that I wanted to sell, so I created a one-page ad called "Finally a Chronograph that Keeps Up with the Amazing Walt Stack." That ad sold tens of thousands of watches and started The Sharper Image. Eventually, The Sharper Image had 200 retail stores, a monthly catalog, a robust online web store, and 4,000 employees. Revenues approached a billion dollars. We became a publicly-traded stock company on Nasdaq under the stock symbol SHRP. I learned to relate to analysts and investors, and I also learned that stock analysts vary greatly in their understanding of a particular company's future success. Just because they are analysts does not mean they're accurate in predicting the future!

At The Sharper Image, for 40 years, I screened or created hundreds of products and looked at hundreds of product ideas. This was a great learning experience because I saw what sold and what didn't. Some ideas succeeded wildly; some didn't sell well. Fortunately, I had a talent for identifying trends and products that would succeed.

After I left The Sharper Image in 2006 and began indulging my passion for full-time investing in stocks, I applied the same talent to choosing individual stocks. Which companies were going to succeed? Which stories should I invest in? This is a talent, and it can be developed over time by watching, investing, and seeing what works and what doesn't. As an alternative, you can rely on someone else's talent to pick stocks, especially if you're just getting started.

Intelligence means you can evaluate trends based on the available information. You do not need to be a genius, but it helps a lot to read, study, and absorb. An intelligent person is someone who has the capacity to respond to mental challenges, deducing logic, inferring hints, and understanding complex subject matter upon explanation. This is a real asset in choosing stocks and equally important in analyzing market movements.

I spend at least three hours a day reading, just enjoying the news and especially the financial news. From reading these various news sources, I can intelligently put together an analysis of trends. For example, in 2021, we were coming out of the COVID-19 lockdown year. So, that was a good time to invest in reopening stocks, an airplane manufacturer like Boeing, a ride service like Lyft, a theme park like Disney, or an airline like Southwest.

It was a year that was the tipping point for electric cars. Although they are still less than 5 percent of all car sales in the US, the major manufacturers have all said they are phasing out gas cars in the next 15 years. This creates an opportunity for us to invest in the electric car revolution. Tesla (TSLA) is, of course, the single biggest player in electric cars, but there are also new players like

NIO Inc. (NIO) and LI (Li Auto Inc.) and charging station stocks, like Plug Power (PLUG) and Blink (BLNK), and Hydrogen players like Ballard Power (BLDP). By reading and thinking, you will see these news stories, as you analyze them, you'll see opportunities where to invest.

Knowledge is essential because you cannot make sound investment decisions without some familiarity and understanding of the facts. What is happening with a particular company and the markets? Knowledge is sometimes experiencing the product or service firsthand. Other times it is reading an article or review, watching an interview with the CEO of the company on CNBC, or following a chat board or comments section.

There is no "one way" to get this knowledge. For example, my knowledge of Tesla was a combination of first-hand experience with the car and reading about Tesla.

A lot of knowledge comes from digesting the different opinions on stocks. I read online articles on sites like CNBC.com, MarketWatch.com, and SeekingAlpha.com. I also watch a lot on CNBC's financial news channel and especially *Mad Money* with Jim Cramer in the afternoon. I also subscribe to *Action Alerts PLUS* for a few hundred dollars a year.

What you find is a wealth of opinion, and much of it is contradictory. Your mission is to read and digest it so that you come to a conclusion regarding a particular company's future success. Combining your intelligence with some knowledge of the field gives you an advantage.

Common sense may be the rarest quality; as it is said, "Common sense is uncommon!"

Sometimes common sense is the most important quality of all these attributes, as we work on earning our 50% per year return. I really like this Wikipedia definition: "The first type of common sense, good sense, can be described as the knack for seeing things as they are." Isn't that the objective when investing—"to see things as they are"? There is some hype and some fluff in company stories or some hope and promise that may or may not materialize. We need to be able to separate the "wheat from the chaff" as we choose where to invest our money.

This common sense comes into play when markets are moving irrationally. You want to understand that sometimes the market is not behaving rationally, and *that* can create opportunity.

The "herd instinct" is a real factor in market moves. The market lurches up or down, sometimes far more than what the situation might dictate. So if you keep a level head, you have an advantage over other traders. Don't be afraid to buy when others are fearful; that might be the smartest thing you do!

Lastly, you need a *bias toward action*. It is so important to take action when you see an opportunity. Failure to do so happens all the time. You see an opportunity, and you think about it, and then you think some more, and eventually, the opportunity has passed you by.

However, It needs to be said that we don't want to jump in too hastily or make investments without some thought.

You will hear many times from others, or experience it yourself, a situation where you had the thought to invest but decided to wait. Then the stock moves up, and you kick yourself. "I thought about it but didn't do it." That happened with Tesla in 2020. I have a friend who bought a new Tesla Model 3 in 2019. When I ran into him in December 2020, he mentioned that he loved the car and had thought about buying the stock but didn't buy in for some reason. He said, "I could have bought two more top-of-the-line Tesla cars if I had bought the stock. I wish I had."

Tesla stock went up 700% in 2020. No wonder he wishes he had bought more stock!

IS OUR SELF-IMAGE TIED TO OUR MARKET PERFORMANCE?

I realize we shouldn't judge ourselves or value our person on how our stock investments perform. There are so many qualities that make up your persona. For me, however, it is a significant part of my self-esteem, and I think of myself as measured intellectually in part by my performance in the stock market. It makes me feel that I am succeeding at my chosen endeavor and also making money, which lets me support myself, and also my charitable endeavors.

I hope that I have plenty of other values and components to my personality, such as being a good parent, being an ethical person, being charitable and kind, a person who is dedicated to helping the environment, and other qualities. But let's not overlook that having more money lets us do some of these things even better.

You will find that as you increase your portfolio, you will have more confidence in other areas as well. You will feel better about yourself, you will have money to spend on yourself and your family, and money to support charitable endeavors.

For me, it has been satisfying to see the profits add up, and also to spend some. It's down-to-earth stuff, as simple as improving the landscaping in my yard (that can get expensive!) or buying an Airstream RV. The money lets me do this, and spending it doesn't hurt my budget. I made it this year in the market, and there's plenty left over. You can do this too. It is fun trading, it is fun seeing the profits add up, and it is fun spending some of it. And because you did it yourself—you earned it—you can enjoy and feel good about it. No guilt required—it is your money, and you made it.

This has been a great experience. Getting results that average over 100 percent a year for the past four years does a lot to make me feel good about my performance and really does a lot to give me the extra money to do my favorite projects. I want you to have this positive experience also.

THIS STRATEGY WORKS FOR BEGINNERS AND EXPERIENCED INVESTORS

You could make so many other moves, from the basics of buying stock to making fancy options trades. But after years of doing this, I find the best and most productive trades are just these two: one is to sell put options on a stock, with an expiration date one or two weeks out; the other is to buy LEAPs, or long-dated call options on a stock, with an expiration date two years out. This approach is for people who are beginning investors, novices, or even seasoned traders who haven't done options trading before or don't really know exactly what they're doing with options trading.

Our investment strategy is not mathematically complicated. You will need a calculator and an understanding of basic math. That's about it. It's a very basic strategy, but it works. If you follow the guidelines explained in these chapters, you will achieve extraordinary returns.

Ideally, you would want to have at least $100,000 available to invest. There is not much opportunity to sell puts with that amount, but you can place some long-dated call option bets. Of course, you can buy some individual shares of stock, but I'm much more enthusiastic about long-call options compared to stock.

When you start making these trades, if you are a newcomer to options, expect that it will be confusing at first, and you will make mistakes. I know because this is what happened to me. Occasionally I would enter an order incorrectly, maybe sell when I meant to buy, or get the price wrong, or something. It's because it is new that it takes a while to understand and execute smoothly. Go slow at first, especially when putting in your orders, and double-check them. It is just all part of the learning process, and eventually, you will be a really good trader!

KEY POINTS FROM CHAPTER 1

1. Trading is fun! When you become personally involved with your investments daily and control them with an online trading platform, you have the opportunity to wake up with anticipation and excitement.

2. The Sharper Investor is someone with talent, intellect, knowledge, common sense, and a bias toward action.

3. You do not need to be a genius, but it helps a lot to be able to read, study, and absorb information. Put your intelligence into action by evaluating trends based on the information available to you.

4. Take action when you see an opportunity. Failure to do so happens all the time. You see an opportunity, and you think about it, and then you think some more, and eventually, the opportunity has passed by.

5. Make online trades slowly at first, especially when putting in your orders, and double-check them every time. New traders make some mistakes at the beginning.

CHAPTER 2

THE BASICS

love using *Investopedia.com* to look up trading-related information. If you have any questions about the terms I use in this book, I encourage you to use Investopedia. com as a resource for quick clarification. It has excellent information on options too.

Here's a great example from Investopedia on stocks.

- A stock is a form of security that indicates the holder has proportionate ownership in the issuing corporation.

- Corporations issue (sell) stock to raise funds to operate their businesses. There are two main types of stock: common and preferred.

- Stocks are bought and sold predominantly on stock exchanges, though there can be private sales as well, and they are the foundation of nearly every portfolio.

- Historically, they have outperformed most other investments over the long run.[3]

Remember, we are all at different places on the learning curve, so you will always benefit by pulling in multiple sources of information.

Way back when I was a college senior at Yale, I started trading gold commodities. I thought it was easy to watch the trends and figure out a time to buy or sell. I went into my local brokerage office, and back then, you would sit in chairs and watch a projection of the "tape" across a screen. These were a low-tech version of what you see now as a ticker at the bottom of your television screen on CNBC.

At first, I did make some profits, and that gave me the confidence to continue. It was great fun, as I loved guessing the movements of gold and trying to stay "in the green," that is, to remain profitable and avoiding ending up "in the red," which is a loss.

---

3 Adam Hayes. "Stock," *Investopedia*, May 22, 2021, www. investopedia.com/terms/s/stock.asp.

After a few months, I had more losses than wins, and it began to dawn on me that just having a hunch, or guessing which way a stock might move, was not going to be a winning formula. So, I took my losses and decided to rethink my strategy. Perhaps there was a better way to trade! So I stepped back and looked at everything from the bottom up. I started with the basics.

WHAT KINDS OF STOCKS?

We start with the premise that the stock market is a good place, in general, to invest your money over time. When I say stock market, I refer to publicly traded stocks listed on the New York Stock Exchange or Nasdaq. These are publicly traded stocks. They're liquid. You can sell or buy them with a click.

That's all I'm talking about—publicly traded stocks. There are undoubtedly many investment vehicles, but we limit ourselves to publicly traded stocks on listed exchanges, traded every day on sites like E*TRADE and TD Ameritrade.

I concentrate primarily on the United States. I don't often get interested in foreign stocks because it's hard to get accurate information about them, and the auditing standards differ in every country. A few large Chinese companies interest me, such as Alibaba, and I have invested in the Chinese electric car company, Nio. These two are listed in the US market at E*TRADE, so they are easily purchased.

It is virtually impossible to buy shares in companies that are not listed in the US. I did that once with Hyundai Motor Company of South Korea before it was listed in the US. Their cars were just coming onto the American market in 1988 with the new Sonata model, and I was impressed with the styling and performance; and the car price was 10 percent less than competing models from Toyota and Honda. I called my Charles Schwab broker and arranged to invest in their stock, which was only listed in South Korea. My investment was about $500,000, and it doubled over the next couple of years. When I wanted to sell it and take my profit, it took weeks, and Schwab charged me roughly 3 percent or $30,000 to make this trade! That is an unacceptably high commission, and I decided not to bother with investments like this in the future.

It was a big and expensive hassle, though profitable, but now I only invest in US stock exchange-listed companies. If you keep your investments to companies listed in the US, you have some assurance that the reporting is accurate and the accounting is done to a certain standard. They can be bought and sold easily with no commission or a very low commission.

ARE STOCKS A BETTER INVESTMENT THAN REAL ESTATE?

One question that gets asked regularly is, "I could buy a house, and I could rent it out, or I could buy a teardown or a fixer-upper, and I could fix it up, and I could sell it for a profit. Should I?" Well, I've tried that, and it didn't turn out very well.

Here's the problem. Unless you're a professional contractor, you're buying services at retail. By that, I mean that if you need new carpets, you're paying retail. You're not in the carpet business. If you need a roof, you're paying retail. You're not a roofer. If you need windows, you're buying them at retail. You're not a window company.

So what happens is you bought this property, put this money in at retail, and now you're trying to either rent it at a price that pays you a profit, or you want to sell it, flip it, and make a profit. But it doesn't usually work out that way. What usually happens is you break even at best. There are some other expenses as well. Like when selling a house, you could pay the realtor up to 6 percent. So on a $300,000 house, you're out $18,000 right away just for the real estate commission. The seller pays the real estate commission. You have property taxes in the meantime while you're holding the property. It just doesn't usually work out. Take my advice on this. I have tried it a couple of different ways. Unless you are a professional house remodeler, it is a challenging way to make money.

If you did it professionally—you bought large apartment buildings, had a lot of money, and had professional management—that can be a profitable business. That's different from the average investor saying, "I'm going to buy a house, fix it up, flip it, or rent it."

But an even bigger problem with real estate is the lack of liquidity. I am a huge believer in liquidity.

What do I mean by that? That if you have a portfolio of E*TRADE, you could sell it today and have the money tomorrow or the next day for sure in cash, but if you have a house and you want to sell it, you might have your money in a month or two or six months. It takes a lot of time and some aggravation. It's so different clicking at E*TRADE and liquidating something into cash within 24 hours compared to selling a house. That can take months to get your money out.

I'll save you a lot of pain and aggravation by saying unless you are born into a family that's been in the business of building apartment buildings for years and knows exactly what they're doing, you're probably not easily going to make money in real estate. I'm sure it can be learned, I'm sure somebody can do it, but that is rare. You will have so much more fun and make money so much more quickly by putting it into an E*TRADE account.

So let's avoid investing in the fixer-upper housing market for now, unless you buy a home for your primary residence and need some home-improvement projects to keep you busy.

GETTING STARTED WITH AN ONLINE BROKER

How should you choose an online trading platform? The most crucial factor is to look for an online trading platform with low commissions, where you can click your mouse and make a trade.

I like and use E*TRADE. I think it's great. Others are good, like TD Ameritrade or Interactive Brokers. I don't like Schwab for various reasons, such as how their operating system works, but it might work for you.

It is straightforward to open an account today; just go online and register. That's all there is to it. You can begin with a small deposit before depositing additional funds from other brokerage accounts or cash accounts.

I suggest that if you do not have an online portfolio already, like E*TRADE or TD Ameritrade, that you consider closing out—selling all your conventional stock positions and moving the cash to E*TRADE or a similar platform, and starting fresh. You will learn and enjoy how to place trades yourself, and having it all in cash to start will be a significant advantage. This will set you up for success for several reasons.

First, it's often difficult to track the gain or loss of existing positions after transferring to an online platform. The extra math and tracking can be cumbersome and time-consuming.

Next, one of the things I love is watching my money grow based on the trades I make. Knowing how much you started with makes it very easy to see how your trading impacts your account. There is a subtle feeling of empowerment, responsibility, and accountability from being 100 percent engaged in how your money grows. You get to take all of the credit! And, you will most likely experience an adrenaline rush when you begin to trade!

Lastly, you may be depositing multiple sources of income into your online platform. If that is the case, try to begin with one grand total in cash so that you can watch your money grow and measure it more easily. Remember, you don't have to have active trades with all the money you put into your account. However, as you learn more about selling puts, you will find that having extra cash in your account will support you in making trades that will help you increase your returns on a weekly basis. I'll discuss having extra cash in your account in more detail in our chapter about selling puts.

However, let me point out that if you cash out (sell) from a conventional brokerage account with big unrealized gains, you may trigger realized taxable gains. You need to evaluate the tax consequences for your situation.

HOW TO GET APPROVED FOR OPTIONS TRADING

Next, it's time to get approved for options trading. To be approved to trade options, you apply online inside your trading platform after you have an active investment account. You can apply by "checking off" certain boxes and choosing specific criteria in drop-down boxes that indicate your level of experience.

If you search on the web to help you with options trading approval guidelines, you won't find a list of criteria you can duplicate to guarantee approval for options trading. I believe this is because regulatory requirements prohibit trading platforms from going into detail on their sites. And, I imagine, the criteria differ slightly by platform, based on the target audience.

Each online trading platform has its own algorithms that are set up based on various factors, including numbers of trades per year, years of experience, and account balance. If you read trading forums on the web, you'll probably find traders who say that trading platforms don't fact check the information you give them but rather accept your statements at face value, though I don't really know.

If the information meets the broker's criteria for qualification, they will most likely accept your reported information as written and give you approval. Most trading platforms want to see that you reported information, indicating you have some prior experience and are comfortable with a higher risk level than the more conservative approach. So look for terms like "speculative" for your trading goal. The platforms are looking for an indication that you have options trading experience, both in years and the number of filled option trades per year. Again, no course or certification standardizes qualifications for options trading, just unpublished algorithms that suggest the applicant has experience in higher-risk trading situations.

Having said all that, it is worth noting that, in my opinion, buying call options has limited risk. You can only lose what you put up at the beginning when you buy the call. Selling put options is quite different. Your potential loss is unlimited. So you do not want to sell put options until you get some experience and understand what you are doing. You don't want to get into a situation where you have a big loss!

The good news about this is that big money is made in buying call options, and that is where your potential loss is limited to what you put up at the beginning, so that is safer for someone who is just getting into investing. It is a fairly easy process to get approved for buying calls.

DAY TRADER? SHORT TERM? LONG TERM?

Now you might wonder, are we "day trading"? Day trading is when you buy and sell on the same day. By the time the market's closed at the end of the day, you've cashed out and gone flat; that is, you have no money exposed to the market overnight because you closed out your positions by the end of the day and added up your winnings or losses. In other words, you have no open positions.

The answer is "no, we're not day trading." I don't believe in the logic of day trading, which is to watch the moves in a particular stock or index and guess whether it is going up or down. I don't know or understand how people do it, and that's not what we are doing.

Do I ever have some positions that are "short-term"? Absolutely. The most common one is selling put options that are one week or two weeks out. Those only have a life of a few days or a week or two weeks. Then the put options expire, and the trade is over. It is very short term: one week or less.

I've tried going out longer for the expiration date, and it has not proved to be a successful strategy. That is too long a time period to be exposed; and if you get into a loss position, it is discouraging and costly to be looking at the loss for weeks or months until the put expires. After lots of experimentation, I've concluded that you do not want to sell puts that are further out.

That is the only short-term trading that I do. Selling put options is comparable to a baseball game, where you are banging out singles every week. It is not a home run. It is rarely even a double, and never a triple or a home run. By that, I mean, we will make a small amount of money, though it is every week, and then the trade is over, and you get your cash back, which is important.

It is very satisfying to make $10,000, or $100,000 every week, and then the trade is over. Unfortunately, it is a taxable event, so if you are in a taxable account like I am, you are accumulating short-term realized gains that will be taxable each year. Of course, if you are in an IRA or a non-taxable account, you are not paying current income tax on the gains, so you have an advantage there.

Are we long-term investors? Well, yes, we are. We stay long invested sometimes because we have gotten ourselves into a great position, with some unrealized profits already accumulated in the position. I suggest that if you still like the company's story, don't sell it. Just hold onto it. Let it ride, if for no other reason than to avoid paying the income tax you would owe if you realized the gain.

"THE BEST HOLDING
PERIOD IS FOREVER"

I have some positions—like Apple, Tesla, Amazon, Home Depot, and Restoration Hardware—that I have held for 10 or 15 years or more. My approach is to hold for the long term if there is a large unrealized gain and if I still believe in the company. That way, there is no taxable event, and the stock position continues to grow in value. *The Motley Fool*, an investing advice forum, says it this way: "Let me be clear: The best holding period is forever, especially for high-quality companies that are well-equipped to thrive for many decades to come."[4]

On the other hand, if you don't continue to believe in the company's strategy or execution, that is a different situation, and then you want to sell it and cash out.

Many advisors give the advice, and I can't argue with it, that if you have a position that has gone up a lot, then sell some, perhaps half, and keep the rest. The idea is that you recover your initial investment, and now you are just letting the profits ride or "playing with the house's money." Although I prefer to let the

---

4   Anders Bylund. "2 Reasons Why I Sold Some of My Tesla Stock," *The Motley Fool*, Jan. 16, 2021, www.fool.com/investing/2021/01/16/2-reasons-why-i-sold-some-of-my-tesla-stock.

entire position stay invested if I like the company, either approach is a good one.

It is a judgment call, and you take into account your cash needs, how much you like the stock, whether you think it might go up further, whether you are in a taxable account, or whatever other factors you see that might affect it. You can decide which you prefer based on your temperament and tolerance for risk.

KEY POINTS FROM CHAPTER 2

1. The Sharper Investor Winning Formula limits us to publicly traded stocks on listed exchanges, which are traded every day on sites like E*TRADE and TD Ameritrade.

2. Liquidity is one main difference between real estate investments and trading in the stock market. And, I think the stock market is much more profitable unless you are a professional real estate developer.

3. Activate your account on an online trading platform with zero or low commissions, where you can go online, click, and make a trade. E*TRADE is my preferred platform.

4. After you have an active investment account, apply online, inside your trading platform, to be approved for options trading.

LET'S TALK ABOUT OPTIONS

WHAT IS OPTIONS TRADING?

Options trading may seem complicated or over-whelming. You may have questions like: What's the difference between an option and a stock? Why is there more potential profit in trading options than there is in stock? We'll cover everything you need to know about options in this chapter, but let's start by turning to Investopedia for some basic information.

The information below shows you how easy it is to research and will help you get started with the basics as we launch into Chapter 3.

- "An option is a contract giving the buyer the right, but not the obligation, to buy (in the case of a call) or sell (in the case of a put) the underlying asset at a specific price on or before a certain date.

- "People use options for income, to speculate, and to hedge risk.

- "A stock option contract typically represents 100 shares of the underlying stock."[5]

YOU'VE PROBABLY BEEN TOLD OPTIONS ARE RISKY

Most people have read or heard that trading options is a risky strategy. I guess the reason for that is that options are "leveraged," meaning that you can make more, or lose more, than just buying or selling stocks.

So, we can agree that when you have leverage that allows you to lose more or make more, it is somewhat riskier.

However, we can't overlook the true adage that "risk equals reward."

So, if you want to increase your investment returns, you have to step out of your safe zone and take on more risk.

---

5   Lucas Downey. "Essential Options Trading Guide," *Investopedia*, March 2, 2021, www.investopedia.com/options-basics-tutorial-4583012.

Let's use our intelligence and common sense to manage the risk so that you end up with a good result. Are options risky? Perhaps, but not for me, and you will manage these so that it is not that risky for you.

Here's an example:

If you bought a $100 share of stock, you could lose how much? It could go down 30%, in which case, you lose $30. Say it goes down 50%, you lose $50.

What about the call option in comparison? Well, you fixed the loss the day you bought the option.

Let's use the same $100 stock example, but imagine you bought a call option for $18 instead, with a strike price of $125.

All you can lose is the $18 you paid for the call option. Instead of the stock going down 30% and you losing $30, you only lose $18. That's all you put up. Instead of losing $50 if the stock goes down 50%, all you can lose is $18.

Call options are safer than stocks when you look at it that way, because you've capped your loss the day you initiated the position. You put up your $18 for a call option, and that's all you can lose.

When you think a trade through and use your intelligence, along with what you have read about the stock, and combine that with your actual experience with the company, you minimize your risk. This is key to the principles of *The Sharper Investor Winning Formula*.

KEEP UNREALIZED GAINS
FOR THE LONG TERM

What is an unrealized gain? I talk about this a lot because it's important to understand the tax ramifications of holding versus selling. If a position is "unrealized," that means you still have it in your portfolio. You have not closed it out. You have done only one-half of the complete trade. You've bought it, but you haven't sold it. Because you haven't sold it, the gain is unrealized.

It's important to know that unrealized gains are not taxed. Until you realize a gain by selling it and completing the transaction, there is no taxable event. If you cash out the position by selling, and realize the gain and pay the tax, you're going to have a lot less money left at the end of the year, unless you're in a non-taxable account, like a retirement account.

On the other hand, if you let the money run, your unrealized gains are not taxed unless the laws change. If you do end up with some call options that are doing really well, you might continue to hold them to expiration with a high positive gain percentage. You could, of course, sell them any time and realize the profit. My account is taxable, so I hold them to expiration. Then what happens is that on expiration day, the call option is exercised, and I buy the stock for the strike price. For that reason, I often become a long-term investor. If I have a position with nice unrealized gains already in it, I will let it run, and not sell and pay income tax. I'll let them run forever unless the company story changes and I no longer have confidence in the company.

WHAT ABOUT THE OTHER OPTION STRATEGIES?

There are lots of other ways to make trades with options. They have crazy names like Bear Spread, Short Straddle, Short Strangle, Ratio Call Spread, Long Butterfly, Long Condor, Box Spread, and others. If you want to learn more about trading options, you'll find at least 26 different strategies. My favorite "cheat sheet" is the PDF from the Australian Securities Exchange. Find it at *www.asx. com.au*.

However, I don't personally use any of them. We're going to use the simplest, most basic strategies. This is to buy a call option or sell a put option. This is so simple. You don't need a complicated strategy, and you don't need any of those fancy names. If somebody tries to make you feel inadequate because you don't know how to do a lot of options trades, ignore them. This strategy is so much simpler.

KEY POINTS FROM CHAPTER 3

1. A stock option contract typically represents 100 shares of the underlying stock.

2. Buying call options, in my view, is safer than buying stocks because your loss, should it turn out to be a loss, is limited to the amount you invested the day you initiated the position, and that amount is a fraction of what the stock would have cost you.

3. When a stock is rising, buy call options instead of buying the stock because the option and the stock will grow at about the same rate, but less money is needed to initiate the call position, and yet you control the same number of shares of stock.

4. Unrealized gains are not taxed. In a taxable account, options can be held until the expiration. Then, when the call option is exercised, the stock is bought for the strike price (+ the premium paid), and it shows up in your portfolio as an unrealized gain, and there is no taxable event. This is important for managing your income taxes.

CHAPTER 4

CHOOSING THE RIGHT STOCKS

"Buy the right stocks" seems like obvious advice, but it's a key part of my success. So how do you pick the stocks that are right for you?

My strategy is to choose companies that I understand and that are doing well in their field, especially those who are first movers or the dominant player. I couldn't care less what the financials are behind it. Certainly, there are people who are value investors, and all they care about are the financials behind it. I respect that, and I admire them for their skill, but that's not what we're doing.

We're selling puts, betting the stock price won't go down too much by Friday, or we're buying two-year-out long-dated calls because we think the company will do better in the future. And that has nothing to do with the numbers behind it. It's more of a sales trend. It's more an understanding of what the product is, what the company's doing, and what their market position is. We highly value the company's market strategy, how their stock has behaved during the past year, and whether we think the strategy will continue to work for the company.

What am I looking for in choosing a stock? First, I find a stock that has a story I understand. This is as simple as realizing that Domino's makes and delivers pizza, has the best digital app, and offers the best delivery in the business. Understanding the company's basic mission is good; knowing what makes them special is even better. That is what gives you an edge. One thing to know is that Domino's makes and delivers pizza, but the edge is that they have been the leader in mobile app sales for pizza. They are much more advanced in digital compared to their competition.

This is the important point: We want to understand the company we are investing in, and we want to understand their advantage. What's making them stand out compared to their competition?

A lot of people are just day trading, just watching stocks go up and down but not following the news. Other people turn their money over to a money market fund or a broker, and they're not paying much attention to the specific news, such as Boeing getting new orders for jet planes today. But you, because you're reading, you're thinking about the news. This is good for the brain too! It will keep your mind sharp. I think too many people retire and don't use their brains enough. This is a great way to keep your brain active and healthy, and hopefully, make a lot of money at the same time!

To figure out the best stocks, we've got to build up our knowledge of different companies and then use our intellect, common sense, and talent to analyze that knowledge.

Here are six fundamentals I use to educate myself and maintain my market knowledge:

1. Read financial news.
2. Look for market dominance.
3. Watch the actions of market leaders.
4. Keep an eye on CEO interviews.
5. Follow current events.
6. Buy companies you know and love.

READ FINANCIAL NEWS

The more information you can get, the better your decisions will be. The more you read, the more you learn. I would suggest devoting two or three hours a day at least to reading. And I'm going to include, along with reading, watching CNBC financial news or FOX business news on television, or listening to it on XM/Sirius Radio.

Spending several hours a day or more gives you a leg up on everyone else. I subscribe and pay for CNBC Pro, *Action Alerts PLUS*, and MarketWatch.com. If you did just these three, you would have plenty of information, so long as you combine it with your own personal experiences.

I love Jim Cramer; he is one of my favorite stock gurus. He hosts a show called *Mad Money* on CNBC at 6 p.m. Eastern time. One of the services that Jim Cramer has created is the stock newsletter, called *Action Alerts PLUS*. This is a paid subscription to an "investing club," which includes weekly market analysis and their favorite stock picks. It is very inexpensive for what you get. It is an incredible resource and boasts a hard-working team that does great research.

I learned in October 2021 that Jim is leaving *Action Alerts PLUS* and starting a new investment club at CNBC. My plan is to continue my subscription to *Action Alerts PLUS*, and also join his new investment club at CNBC. For the time being, the CNBC investing club is a free sign-up, so you should join it too.

Over time, I have found these to be excellent resources for stock picks. There are others, to be sure, but these are excellent. If you just stick to the number one picks on *Action Alerts PLUS*, you will do well. These weekly stock picks are divided up by a rating of one, two, or three, with the number one rating representing stocks they recommend buying right now.

Here is an example of their analysis of one of the "number ones" for the week of June 18, 2021, which is Amazon, also one of my favorite stocks:

Amazon (AMZN)
$3,496.95; 47 shares; 4.4%;
Sector: Consumer Discretionary

WEEKLY UPDATE: Analysts at Jefferies added AMZN to their "Franchise Pick List," swapping the name in for GOOGLE and commenting that "fundamentals are likely to benefit from increased e-comm adoption and faster growth at its highest margin businesses. Our proprietary survey points to a permanent increase in online consumption, with 63 percent of respondents continuing to spend more online even after restrictions were lifted. In addition, AMZN's stock has lagged since mid-2020, w/ valuation now at a ~10 percent discount to its historical average."
1-Wk. Price Change: 4.19%;
Yield: 0.00%

INVESTMENT THESIS: We believe upside will result from Amazon's continued Commerce dominance, AWS' continued leadership in the public cloud space, and ongoing growth of the company's advertising revenue stream, which feeds off Amazon's eCommerce business. Additionally, we believe profitability will continue to improve as AWS and advertising account for a larger portion of total sales as both these segments sport higher margins than the eCommerce operation. And while we believe the increasing share of the revenue from these higher-margin businesses will be key to driving profitability longer-term, we believe margins on eCommerce stand to improve as the company's infrastructure is further built out and economies of scale further kick in. The embedded call option is that management is always looking to enter a new space and generate new revenue streams.
Target Price: Reiterate $4,000;
Rating: One

RISKS: High valuation exposes the stock to volatile swings, eCommerce has exposure to slower consumer spending, competition, management is not afraid to invest heavily, potential headwinds resulting from new eCommerce regulation in India,

> management is not scared to invest aggressively
> for growth, which can at times cause volatile
> reactions as near-term concerns arise relating to
> the impact on margins.

Action Alerts PLUS mentions several points for this pick that catch my attention. First, he mentions that a prominent analyst has chosen Amazon to replace Google in his picks. Then he goes on to point out that Amazon is lagging its historic price level, which suggests it might be a good time to buy in ("buy low and sell high"). He reiterates some reasons why their volume and margins will probably improve. All this gives me the confidence to continue to buy into the Amazon story, which I already love.

I sell put options on Amazon every week, because I have confidence that in general, it is heading higher.

This is what I often do: If I start to like a company's stock, I cross-check it and see if by chance it is one of the same stock names that *Action Alerts PLUS* chose. If it is on both our lists, then I feel highly confident that it is a winner.

When you're reading the financial news, here are some trends to keep an eye on:

LOOK FOR MARKET DOMINANCE:
TASER (AXON)

The people that invented the TASER twenty-five years ago created a product designed to provide an alternative to conventional lethal weapons. Now, they dominate the market. Every police person you meet has a TASER weapon on their utility belt. And I'm a great believer that, when you're the market leader, that's a huge advantage.

In the past five years, Axon Enterprises, which manufactures TASER devices, has also become the market leader in police body cameras. They sell not only physical cameras but also a huge digital platform that works with body cameras. Sure enough, the company has done great. Back in 2018, the stock was as low as $20. In March 2020, it dipped along with the market to $57. In the spring of 2021, the stock took a dip, from $160 to $141. Even with the dips, we can see that the overall trend is that this stock has risen tremendously in value. As of August 30, 2021, it was up to $193!

What's the moral of the story? You can pick a good stock by researching the product and the company, noticing that it's the market leader, and believing that police cameras are an important thing in the future, which I think we all agree.

WATCH THE ACTIONS OF MARKET
LEADERS: THOR (THO)

Thor came to my attention when they made news in the past month because they acquired another company.

Thor is the maker of Airstream, those beautiful aluminum trailers that you see regularly. Airstream is a wonderful brand name with iconic products. They added to their brand names by buying Tiffin in December 2020, and Tiffin is the leading and most luxurious maker of big RVs, the bus-sized RVs.

Airstream has also gotten a lot of attention for its new motor coaches which are based on the Mercedes Sprinter chassis. These small motor coaches are only 19 to 24 feet in length. They contain a small kitchen, bathroom with shower, lounge area that converts into a bedroom at the press of a button, and many features like solar panels and lithium-ion batteries.

These motor coaches are so popular in 2021 that the waitlist time is six months—for a $200,000 vehicle! I wanted to see what all the excitement was about, so I found a 2020 model with only 8,000 miles on it that looked and checked out to be like brand new. Here's a photo. That's my Giant Schnauzer, Max, standing beside it. After driving it for the first month, and taking a couple of trips, I was impressed and still am!

The stock hit a low of about $32 in March of 2020, and it was about $119 in August 2021, so it's more than tripled since March 2020. But it's not just the momentum of the stock price that's interesting.

What's interesting to me is I know Tiffin is a famous brand name in RVs. I know that Airstream is an iconic brand and everyone loves Airstream trailers, and they're fabulous. When you combine the two best brand names in the business, at a time when people are going more and more into traveling and camping with RVs, I think that's a terrific concept. And it's nothing more complicated than just knowing the brand names and knowing there's a trend here toward more RVs.

You might ask, "Well, what about all the financial analysis behind this? How do I know the merger makes good sense financially? Do I know what the price-to-earnings ratio is? Have I researched their balance sheet? Do I know their enterprise value?" And the answer is, I don't know. That isn't part of my strategy.

My strategy is to identify that RVs are a hot trend right now, and that the leading brand is Airstream, and Tiffin is a leading brand in large RVs, and that the wait-list for the popular Airstream models is six months, and that these two brand names just merged. The stock chart has tripled during the past 12 months, so the momentum is in its favor. This seems like a good time to buy long-dated calls on Thor.

KEEP AN EYE ON CEO INTERVIEWS: SALESFORCE (CRM) AND MARK BENIOFF

Occasionally, I see a CEO company interview on CNBC, and I am so impressed with the intelligence and confidence of the CEO, I make an investment in the company based on the interview. I might not know personally what the company's product or service is precisely about in that situation. Salesforce.com is a company like that for me. I like the CEO, Marc Benioff, and I do not know firsthand the specifics of what they do...though I realize it is customer relationship management software.

What I do know is that Marc Benioff has done a terrific job of building Salesforce into a powerhouse, and every quarter he seems to deliver stellar results. When I listen to his regular appearances on CNBC, he gives me the confidence to invest in the company. And the stock has continued to go up, making for a very successful investment whether buying long calls or selling short-dated puts.

FOLLOW CURRENT EVENTS: BOEING (BA)

As you know, Boeing aircraft, one of the greatest companies ever, suffered terribly in 2020. One of their best airplanes, the 737 Max airliner, was grounded, and then the COVID-19 shutdown hit in 2020, curtailing air travel. Boeing had a terrible year, and the stock fell from a high of $439 in 2019, down to a low of $89 on March 19, 2020. That is a huge drop and gives us the thought that it has reached a really appealing price level.

After the stock suffered that huge drop, you might wonder, when is a time to get long again (buying some two-year-out call options) and start averaging in? Then there is some news around January 2021. It was announced that the 737 Max had finally received FAA certification to fly again after two years of governmental review.

And in that same week, the news broke that two major airlines had placed new orders for Boeing airplanes. You have to appreciate that Boeing had not received any airplane orders for the prior two years, and suddenly, they were getting new orders. I'm thinking that the facts are becoming more persuasive: the 737 Max is recertified to fly, and airlines are starting to place orders. The COVID-19 vaccine will probably be successfully rolled out by mid- to late-2021. Boeing is probably going to go up and probably not going to go down anymore. Then it happened again. In June 2021, Boeing got a 200 plane order from United Airlines!

I have been selling put options on BA every week and making money every week, figuring that the stock is heading higher and not likely to go lower for the reasons discussed above. I also bought long-dated calls on Boeing all through the first half of 2021. And what has the stock done? It has recovered from its low of $97 in March 2020 to about $235 in August 2021.

How did I know that Boeing was a good bet? Just reading the news gave me that confidence.

BUY COMPANIES THAT YOU KNOW AND LOVE: CHIPOTLE (CMG)

One of my favorite investing books is *One Up on Wall Street: How to Use What You Already Know to Make Money in the Market* by Peter Lynch. I love this book because he gives you the confidence that if you know a company, if you buy its products, and if you know they are providing a valuable product or service, you should have confidence buying their stock (or call options).

The central theme of his book is that you should choose stocks that you know and understand. In other words, companies that you interact with and understand from personal experience. This was such a strong theme for Peter Lynch, and it has worked so well for me. Whenever I get involved with a company, such as using their product or service, I think of Peter Lynch. His advice has guided me for 40 years to recognize an opportunity for investing.

Consider Chipotle Mexican Grill—what a great company! They had a bad experience with food poisoning around 2015. They continued to have sporadic food episodes, and then they recovered from that, and hired a CEO named Brian Niccol, who had in his most recent job as CEO of Taco Bell made Taco Bell a huge success. At Chipotle, it's still Mexican food, but with much higher quality.

So Brian Niccol is now applying his smart savvy to the Chipotle digital platform, the menu, and the customer experience, which are things he understands and perfected at Taco Bell, but he's doing it in a much higher-quality environment. As a result, Chipotle and the stock have done fabulously. So when I saw that they had hired Brian Niccol, and I saw that they were getting their food safety issues behind them, I knew it was primed for success.

I regularly pick up food to test it out (and enjoy a very tasty lunch). And I can tell you that it is one of the best experiences ever in terms of sanitation, quality of food, taste, value, and the quality of the people that work there.

It's just a great experience, and that translates into a great stock. And this stock has made a fortune for me. CMG hit a 2020 low of $415, and by August 2021, had climbed more than four times to $1,887. What an incredible run this stock has had, and it is still headed higher, in my opinion. I keep going back for lunch, and what impresses me is that they are so organized, and the place is so clean, and the ordering from the app works so well. It seems to be a good league ahead of its competitors in every dimension. Oh, and did I say that I like the food? Try the Sofritas burrito bowl—yum!

WHAT ABOUT TRADITIONAL FUNDAMENTAL VALUES?

You might ask, what about the fundamentals of the company? Do I know or care about the balance sheet, the price-earnings ratio, the current ratio, or the analysts' ratings? Not too much. I do look at them, but in today's market, many stocks have no earnings, which makes the ratio of price to earnings, or PE, totally irrelevant.

Tesla is one of my favorite companies. I started with them in 2011, and they have become one of my best investments. I have made tens of millions of dollars from buying Tesla options and stock that got put to me. And how did this happen? I visited a showroom in 2012, looked at the Model S car, and arranged a test drive. The test drive was a tremendous experience. I couldn't believe how smoothly an electric car could accelerate. I loved the large touch screen panel. Interestingly, there were practically no buttons in the car. One button for the glove box and one for the hazard light, and that was it. Everything else was on the touchscreen. So, I fell in love with the car, and I decided to place an order.

I also started buying some stock in Tesla. The stock was around $35 at that time, and very few analysts were recommending the stock as a hot one to buy. Mostly, the negative analysts were critical of the lack of profits and skeptical that Tesla, and specifically, Elon Musk, were ever going to pull it together, make some money, and deliver many cars. But I had a different view: I was actually in the showrooms, driving the car, and eventually owning a Tesla. As a product guy, I recognized that they were really onto something. The car was ahead of everything else by a wide margin, and the customer service was excellent. I felt it was going to be a winner.

My Tesla experience has been a classic investment success. With Tesla, I knew more about the car and the company than most of those analysts did, though they knew a lot more about the financial ratios. But it did not help them make a sound investment decision in this case.

Think about this. The analyst is probably someone sitting in a room on Wall Street in New York City, and reading some reports. They probably don't own a Tesla, probably haven't driven a Tesla, probably haven't personally

driven a Tesla to a Supercharging station and charged up, probably haven't used the Tesla Mobile Service, and probably don't really know much, hands-on, about the company or its products.

They just know what has been printed in the news. And what happened in hindsight? Most of the analysts totally missed the story and missed the chance to get 10 times their money, or 20 times their money since 2012. This was a classic Peter Lynch stock-picking experience. Buy what you know, buy what you understand, buy what you love.

WHAT ABOUT COMPANIES YOU DON'T KNOW, BUT KEEP HEARING ABOUT?

Bitcoin

I'll never forget the first time I was told to invest in Bitcoin. It was late 2017, I was having the delicious pancake and egg breakfast (super deal!) at an IHOP restaurant, and the waitress was bragging to me about how much money she had made by investing in Bitcoin.

That was the first time I had heard of it. But after this conversation, I decided to buy a very small position. Bitcoin was about $10,000 then. So I ended up with this small position, and very shortly, I watched it drop to $3,000, and it stayed down there for a few years, and then slowly began to move back up, and by July 2020, it was finally back to the same $10,000 that was my entry point. In other words, I held it for about three years to get back to even!

Then, to my amazement, it took off, and by April 2021, it incredibly climbed to $60,000! That is pretty wild to go up 6x in just six months! I didn't make much because my investment was a tiny one, but it was fun to see it go up.

It reminds me of a cliché that you often hear, which is "when the shoeshine boy (or in this case, the waitress) gives you a stock tip, it's probably too late to invest," meaning that if the stock tip has filtered down that far, everyone has already bought in, and there's no one left to buy in. In other words, the price has nowhere to go but down because there are no buyers left.

I wish I had more insight into Bitcoin, Ethereum, and other digital currencies, but I don't. This is an appropriate moment to emphasize again that I limit myself to investing in things I know and understand, and avoid investments that I don't understand. We can make great returns in the stocks we know and understand!

KEY POINTS FROM CHAPTER 4

1. Pick stocks you know and love. Avoid stocks you don't understand. (Once in a while, I buy into a stock story because the analysts are so positive, or the CEO gave such a positive interview—even though I don't really know the stock or company well—CRWD is a good example of this.)

2. Consistently read the news. It will keep your mind sharp. (I spend two to four hours a day.)

3. Pay attention to trends. (It is obvious to me we are moving away from fossil fuels. I definitely would not buy an oil stock!)

4. Use your insight to predict market trends. (You must have noticed that electric vehicles are taking over the car market. And cloud computing and cybersecurity are in the news every day.)

5. Look for market dominance and first movers. Keep an eye on CEO interviews. (I love Tesla, Apple, and Salesforce. They are all ahead of their competition.)

6. Repeat and reuse the six fundamentals I use to educate myself and maintain my market knowledge:
    a. Read financial news.
    b. Look for market dominance.
    c. Watch the actions of market leaders.
    d. Keep an eye on CEO interviews.
    e. Follow current events.
    f. Buy companies you know and love.

CHAPTER 5

CALL OPTIONS

Remember, our strategy uses only two types of options trades: either a call option or a put option. And we do only one type of trade for each: buy a call option or sell a put option.

The big money in our strategy is made in buying call options, and that is where your potential loss is limited to what you put up at the beginning; that is safer for someone who is just getting into investing.

Buying a call option means you pay a premium, and in exchange, you have the privilege to buy a stock at a set price—called the strike price—at the end of two years. In the meantime, you control the stock. By that, I mean you have financial control of as many shares as you bought calls on (the minimum is one contract for 100 shares), even though you do not own the stock until you exercise the call option, which typically happens on the expiration date. But it doesn't make any real difference because owning the option gives you an absolute right to take the shares at the end.

There are two main differences between a call option and a stock: you put up less money for the call option than if you buy the stock, and you do not receive dividends (if a dividend is paid). Otherwise, they act the same.

Here's everything you need to know to get started buying call options.

UNDERSTANDING CALL OPTIONS

The call option is a bet that the stock will rise in value during the time between when you buy and your expiration date. Here is an analogy that demonstrates what a call option is and how it works.

Imagine that there is a piece of land near your home. You drive past it every day. It's a desirable piece of land, maybe 10 acres. It's got a "For Sale" sign on it, and they're asking for a million dollars. But you could perhaps buy an option instead on that piece of land, for $100,000. So instead of putting up a million dollars, which you might not have, you put up $100,000, and because it is a two-year option, you now have two years to think about whether you want to buy the property two years later at the strike price of $1,000,000.

> > 70 < <

If the property happens to double after you bought your option, it is now worth $2 million. You think, "Wow, I like this deal. I'll exercise my option to buy it for a million. I paid a $100,000 premium for the option. So I've got $1,100,000 total into it (purchase price of $1 million plus the option price of $100k), but now it's worth $2 million. Wow. That's terrific."

Think about this. You made a $900,000 gain after exercising the option, for which you paid $100,000 dollars for the option. You exercised the option. All of a sudden, you've got this big gain, an unrealized gain of $900,000, for having put up that $100,000 at the beginning and then later exercising your option after you saw the property go up in value. And you were not forced to exercise the option—you waited until you saw it go up. That is a big advantage compared to paying the entire price upfront because you had the opportunity to watch it for two years and see if it went up or down in value before making your final decision.

And let's look at it another way, which is to analyze the downside. What if the property fell in value so that it is only now worth $500,000? In other words, it lost 50%. If you had your $100,000 option, you could decide to walk away, and you would lose the $100,000 that you paid for that option. Contrast that with what would happen if you had bought the property upfront for $1,000,000.

You would now have a property worth $500,000, and the bottom line to you is that you lost $500,000 on that property.

So for me, I would much rather have the risk of $100,000 for the option, rather than being forced to put up the full purchase price of $1,000,000 to buy it at the beginning. And, when you put up the $100,000 for the option, you kept most of your cash for another investment—you still had the balance of $900,000 for other investments. And, you paid for the privilege of thinking about it for two years, without any obligation to complete the purchase. In other words, you get to think about it and watch it for up to two years before you are forced to make your final purchase decision. It's true, you paid $100,000 up front for that privilege, but it's a valuable privilege that can protect you against the property dropping in value.

So that's how a call option works. You put up a certain amount of money at the beginning, for the privilege of thinking about whether to purchase a stock for up to two years in this case, as we're always going to buy two-year-out options.

CHOOSING CALL OPTIONS

When you buy a call option to purchase a stock, you choose the strike price and the expiration date. We will always pick a price higher than the current price for our strike price, and we always pick an expiration date two years away (sometimes known as LEAPS).

Before you buy a call, wait for a dip in the stock price, which seems to occur every few months, of 10–20%, or close to that. That is the best time to buy a two-year-out call option at a strike price higher than the current stock price.

The actual process of choosing the call option to buy is this:

- Look for an option that is two years into the future. If the stock I am looking at does not go out further than six months, I won't pursue that one.

- Look for a strike price where the option premium for the call is roughly 15–18% of the strike price.

That is the basic idea, with one very important additional leg for our strategy. We only do this with stocks that we wouldn't mind owning! This is one of the most important parts of our strategy. When you think that you have some intuition or opinion about how a stock is moving, but if it is not a stock you would like to own, my advice is to forget it for placing options trades. There is the possibility that you will end up owning some of these stocks, so let's make sure you actually want to own them.

CALL OPTIONS ARE LIQUID

There is one big difference between the example of buying property compared to a call option on a stock. With the property, there is usually no continuing market for the option, no bid or ask. Once you take the option, that is the end of the trade until two years is up.

However, with the call option on the stock, it is very different. The option price is quoted all day, every day, and you can resell your option or cash out and realize your gain or loss and get your money back, anytime you want. So it might happen that some days the stock is up, and your option is up too. And other days, the stock may be down and the option may be down too. It's a big advantage to have daily liquidity on your investment.

PRICE MOVEMENT

I should mention that the price of the call option moves up as the stock price moves up, but with roughly only about 80 percent of the gain that the stock makes. So if the stock goes up $100, the call option might go up $80. That is just an approximate rule of thumb. Sometimes if the stock goes up only a very small amount, the option may not move, as they are independent trades and not in lockstep.

If there is a really wide difference between the stock price and the call option strike price, you will see that the stock moves up some days but the call option doesn't. That is because there is such a wide difference that the traders don't think the gap will ever be close enough to make the option a good bet.

However, if it is still 18 months out, this could change very quickly. If the stock moves up enough to close the gap between the stock price and the call option strike price, you will see the normal ratio return, where the option gets about 80 percent of the gain of the stock price. And if the stock price goes higher than your call strike price, then every dollar the stock goes up will see a corresponding dollar increase in the call option price.

WHY DOES A CALL OPTION MAKE MORE MONEY THAN BUYING THE STOCK?

That's the most basic question anyone could ask about this strategy. Why is a call option better than the stock?

Well, let's look at it this way. Let's say the stock is $100. If you buy the stock for $100, you're out $100. If you buy an option on the stock, let's say for $18, you've only put up $18. That's all you put up. You've got $82 leftover to put into other investments. That's pretty huge, isn't it? Remember, you control the same number of shares.

Let's say the stock doubles over the next year, so your $100 stock is now worth $200. If you had bought the stock, your $100 stock has gone up in value 100%. It has doubled. You made $100, and you have a profit of $100, or 100%. If you had bought the call option instead, you didn't put up $100, you put up $18.

Now you won't quite make the full hundred-dollar appreciation, because when you look at a lot of history, what you find is that call options tend to appreciate in value at about 80% of what the stock does. So, in this example, if the stock goes up $100, your call option might only go up to $80. But you only put in $18, so what is $18 paid compared to $80 earned? It's over a 400 percent return. So in percentage terms, you have a choice. You can buy the stock, and maybe you'll make 100% in a year, or you could buy the call option, and maybe you'll make 400% in a year. Pretty amazing, isn't it? One return is in percentage terms, four times the other. We talked at the beginning about doubling your return. Well, here's four times your return!

One thing to realize—there's only a couple of things that could happen here. If you have a long-dated call option, you could lose the dollars you paid at the beginning for your call, but your loss is limited to what you initially paid. Or you could close the position and cash out anytime during the two years, hopefully for a profit. Or, you could wait till the expiration date, and perhaps end up owning the stock in the green with a nice unrealized profit in your favorite stock.

A REAL-LIFE EXAMPLE OF HOW CALLS MAKE MORE MONEY THAN STOCK

My Tesla experience was very special and has made me literally millions of dollars. It was also a good example of how leverage with call options can make you more money than just buying the stock. The leverage, in this case, is that you are controlling the shares of stock with less cash out of pocket, so the potential return of the investment is higher if it works.

Let me share this real-life mathematical example of why calls are better than buying the stock. We will compare the call options with the stock. This is a true story.

I happened to have bought Tesla stock and bought the same number of shares in calls about the same date. The call options have given me better returns than the stock. I want to demonstrate to you the difference between the two approaches and how it turned out for me. The numbers here are pretty large, but you can reduce it down to represent a smaller investment. It doesn't have to be as large a position as this one—just knock off a few zeroes!

What happened to me was I ended up owning a lot of Tesla stock because it got put to me at the end of a week because I had sold put options. On a Friday, the stock dropped precipitously, and it got put to me, and I kept the stock.

As a result of this put position expiring out of the money, I ended up owning 25,000 shares of Tesla stock. And, at an average price of $86, that was just over a two million dollar investment. That original investment grew to be worth about $22 million dollars as of January 2021. So, roughly $20 million of gain, which is roughly a 900 percent gain. Well, that's tremendous. It is incredible, right? You would love to get a 900 percent return on a stock investment, right?

To have a 900 percent gain in any stock is incredible. However, let's look at the same transaction, but with buying call options instead of stock. By coincidence, I happened to have bought 250 call options on Tesla stock in the same month, which is equivalent to 25,000 shares. I paid $6 per share for the call option. That was about a $150,000 investment. Let's compare that $150,000 investment to the two million dollar investment for the stock.

The call option position controls 25,000 shares. The stock investment is 25,000 shares. It is a true "apples-to-apples" comparison.

A year and a half later, as of January 2021, each position had gone up about $20 million dollars. So, the stock, which cost me a little over two million dollars, had gone up by $20 million, for a 900 percent return. The call option, which cost about $150,000, had also gone up by $20 million, which in percentage terms on the $150,000 investment is a 13,000% return.

Well, no one has ever heard of a 13,000% return, but I've got one here. Each position made $20 million dollars. They both made the same in dollars, but one was a two million dollar investment, and one was a $150,000 investment. Those are big numbers, but you can reduce them down. Instead of being 250 contracts or 25,000 shares, you could have done it for 50 contracts or ten contracts. The percentages would be exactly the same.

The point is, when the stock goes up, you're always much better off if you had bought call options instead of buying the stock, because you're getting about the same growth as in the stock price, but you're putting up a lot less money at the beginning.

BUYING CALL OPTIONS

Let's look at an example of buying long-dated call options, and walk you through the actual mechanics of how to buy a long-dated call option. For this example, let's use one of my favorite companies, Salesforce.com (CRM).

On the E*TRADE Stock Snapshot page on July 20, 2021, the stock happened to be at $239.49. Refer to the example that follows. When I go to the "Options" tab (one of the tabs at the top of the Snapshot page) and click on Options, it gives me a number of dates at the top of the page ranging from next week to two years out. I can click the right arrow to get to the furthest out position. That day, the furthest out was January 20 of 2023. So that was about 18 months out. Remember, I'm a big fan of the longest out expiration date you can trade, which is usually about two years.

So, the stock in this example is $239.79. Next, I click on "Strikes," and select "All." And when I click on All, it shows me all the positions. So I scroll down the page to higher strike prices. I want to get to a number where the price to buy a call option is about 15% of the strike price. At a $250 strike price, for January 2023 (two years out), the option is priced at about $32. Well, that's great. That's about 15 percent of the strike price. So for $32 per share, I can buy a long-dated call option on CRM.

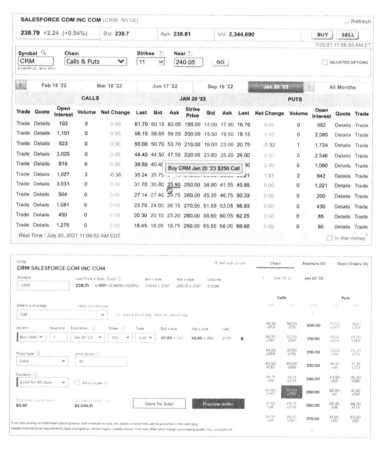

If I bought the stock at $240 a share, that would be an investment of $24,000. But instead of investing $24,000, I can invest $3,200, and control the same 100 shares. To reiterate, we're putting up roughly 15–18% of what it costs to buy 100 shares at $240, and we're getting control of the entire 100 shares.

If the stock goes up, the call option won't capture 100%, but it'll capture about 80% of the gain. You're only putting up about 15% of the money. So, the ratio is working out in your favor. That's the leverage that is going to make these call options work so well.

Going back to my computer screen here, we will click on the $250 strike price. That is only two lines down from the current price. On the options chart, it's going higher than the strike price, but the way the computer screen displays it, it's "lower down." You'll see a bid price, and an ask price. I've learned that you can typically buy it in the middle of the bid and the ask price if you're buying a call.

If you put in the exact "buy" bid price that is showing in the system, you're not going to get it. In this case, the bid is $32, the ask is $33.50. Well, if you put in $32, you will just join the other bidders at $32 and you probably won't get it. If you want to fill that order now, pick a price a little higher. So instead of $32, you put in $32.50 and see what happens. You are splitting the difference between the bid and the ask, and it'll fill at that price usually.

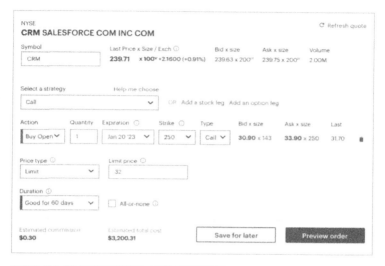

If you want, you can just click "Market Order" and it'll fill somewhere in between the two prices. Or if you want to be really careful and cautious, you could put in the limit bid of $32, then click "Good for 60 Days," and let the order just sit for up to 60 days. The market could drop sometime in the next week or two and you'll get that lower price.

Orders

Open Executed Cancelled Saved Individual fills Expired Rejected All Bond quotes

Account
B1 2020 Annuity Trust -8001

Note: This view does not include saved orders

From date	To date	Symbols	Order number	Order type	Order status	Security type	Results per page	
01/21/2021	01/20/2021		516	All	All	All	20	Apply filters

	Date	Order	Type	Order type	Quantity	Symbol	Price type	Term	Price	Price executed	Status	Links
	07/20/21	516	Option	Buy Open	10	CRM Jan 20 '23 $250 Call	Mkt	Day	Mkt	32.20	Executed	Portfolios

After you successfully execute your order, you are now controlling the stock for about 15 percent of the price of the stock. You also remember we said that when you buy the call option, about $32 in this example, that's all you can lose. Your total investment is capped at that $32 per share. So the stock which is trading around $240 could drop in half, and if it did, you could lose $120 per share if you own the stock. With the call option, it's capped. All you can lose is the $32 per share that you're paying for the option. So in that sense, you're really protecting yourself against a big drop in the stock. You've limited your loss to what you paid initially for that option.

And for full disclosure, I'll mention the alternative point of view, which is that you could pay for the call option price, and eventually lose 100 percent of your investment if the stock falls 50 percent, whereas if you had bought the stock, you would still have 50 percent of your original investment.

LONG-DATED CALLS GIVE THE STOCK TIME TO RISE

Long-dated call options have a built-in safety, which is that your loss is limited to the price you paid for the call. That's all you can lose. That's different from a stock, where the stock could go down 50 percent or 100 percent.

Now it's true, your call option could go down 100 percent because it could expire at the end of two years "out of the money." In other words, it never reaches the strike price, and in that case, it expires worthless and is worth nothing, and you have lost your money.

But I look at it differently—you only put up a small amount of money for it, compared to what you would have put up if you bought the actual stock. You didn't put up 100 percent of the money of the stock price, or on margin, 50 percent. Some people would say, "Yes, the call option is a safer bet because you're only putting up 15 or 20 percent of the total purchase price." Others would say, "No, the call is dangerous because you could lose 100 percent of the option price at the end of the expiration date."

I acknowledge that difference of opinion, and I agree it's possible you could lose 100 percent of your call option investment. However, you're only putting up a small fraction of the value of the stock. In that sense, you're not going to lose 100 percent of the stock value. I guess that's a debatable point, but it's proved to be a fairly conservative investment strategy for me.

It comes down to this simple example: If you put up 15 percent of the stock price for the call option, and then lose it all, you have lost $1,500 on a $10,000 stock investment. However, if you had bought the stock, and it goes down 30 percent, you will lose $3,000. So which would you rather do? It all depends on how much the stock moves, and in which direction. If it goes up, you will be better with the call. If it goes down, it depends on how much it goes down.

Let's look at another example of a long-dated call option trade. We will look at Facebook stock for a two-year call option. The stock is $251 on a particular day I'm looking at the chart. A call for two years out, with a strike price of $275 costs $47.47, which is about 17% of $275, so in other words, you are putting up about 17% of the strike price for the privilege of controlling the entire 100 shares of stock for a two-year period. Instead of putting up $25,100 for 100 shares of the stock, you are putting up $4,747 to control the same number of shares. That is quite a difference!

What are we looking for as a result? We are betting that sometime in the next two years, the stock will move higher than $251 because if it does, the option price will also move higher. Typically it will move about 80% of the stock price movement. If the stock goes up $20, this option price should move up about $16.

Let's do another calculation to see the annualized return. If the $251 stock price goes up in one year by $20, that is an 8% return on your investment. If the $47 call option goes up $16 (80% of the $20), that is a 34% return on your investment. Much better! What if Facebook stock goes up 20 percent? That would take it from $251 to $301. And the call option would go up about $40 (80% of $50), so now the call is at $87 (47 + 40), which is an 85% return. Obviously, you would rather make 85% on your investment, rather than 20%!

It gets a little more complicated because as we approach the last three or four months of the life of the two-year option, there is a time decay effect, which means that the likelihood that the stock will rise to meet the option strike price is running out of time. That will cause the option price you paid initially to slowly be reduced or degraded in value so that at expiration, the value of that option is zero—it expires worthless.

Suppose there is a very wide difference between the stock price and the strike price. In that case, the call will suffer time erosion sooner and be worth less than it would if they were closer together in price because the traders value the call price more highly if there appears to be some chance that the stock might rise to meet the strike price by expiration date.

In other words, you need the underlying stock to rise in value before the option expires worthless.

WHAT TO DO WITH CALL OPTIONS: SELLING OR ROLLING THEM INTO THE STOCK

In my trading career, I've noticed a lot of trends. One, in particular, is related to stocks that tend to move up or down regularly. In a long-dated call option, you will have a time during the first year or 18 months of the option where you will be profitable on the trade, or "in the green." If you find that your option bet is consistently in the red, you might want to concede that it is a losing trade, close it out, and take the loss before it expires worthless at the end of the two years.

One point, about which there is some confusion, is that we do not need to wait for the contract's expiration date. You can take your profit (or loss) anytime you want. There is nothing that compels you to wait two years until the expiration date! That date is really irrelevant until that date arrives.

The option is quoted by the minute, and has instant liquidity, meaning you can sell it and take your profit any day, any moment. Or suppose you want to avoid realizing the gain and paying income tax. In that case, you could wait until expiration, and the call will automatically roll into a new stock position, with the gain still unrealized. No tax is due until you ultimately sell the stock—or perhaps you hold it forever.

The way it works is that you own the call option, and at the time of expiration, it will automatically be exercised, and you will now own the stock instead of the option. So one call contract automatically exercises at expiration, if you are in the green, into 100 shares of stock. You will be credited for whatever gain you have, and it will show up in your portfolio with an unrealized gain. The cash required to accept the stock is also a factor to consider. The call option is cash held up front, but that is less than what is required to take the stock. If there is not enough cash or margin available in your account to accept the stock, you will sell some at a profit, which is not a problem.

WHEN DO CALLS NOT WORK WELL?

The only time you're not very happy with a long-dated call is if the stock is exactly the same price, or a dollar lower, two years later. If the stock has dropped since you initiated your call option, you could be better off with the option than the stock, for the reason that you paid about 18% of the stock price for the option—so if the stock has dropped 30%, you are happy you bought the option instead.

Regarding the stock not moving at all: if you had purchased a call for $15, the stock hasn't moved in two years, and you're going to lose your $15 that has been tied up for two years, making it a $15 loss—this is a typical situation where you'll be unhappy.

However, you can avoid this by choosing stocks that have some volatility to them and move a lot during the year. It is highly unlikely they are not going to move up and down some.

In summary, if you are just starting out, buy call options two years out. You can wait on the put option strategy until you have more cash to work with. Selling put options is riskier because you have an unlimited loss. If you are just starting out, it is more conservative to buy call options. The puts can wait till later in your investing career!

KEY POINTS FROM CHAPTER 5

1. If you are new to investing, only buy call options that are two years out.

2. Buying calls is less risky than selling puts because they have a limited loss.

3. The Sharper Investor values instantly liquid investments. Option prices are quoted all day, every day. You can resell your option or cash out at any time, unlike real estate. Call options are better than the stock itself because you make a lot more money when it goes well, and you use up a lot less cash.

4. Long-dated call options have a built-in safety because your potential loss is limited to the price paid for the call when you initiated it.

CHAPTER 6

PUT OPTIONS

The *Sharper Investor Winning Formula* includes selling put options that are a week, or two weeks, out to expiration. That's it—nothing more complicated than selling the simplest put option.

Selling a put option means you sell someone the right to put the stock to you at your chosen price, called the strike price, at the expiration date you select. I always select an expiration date one or two weeks out.

UNDERSTANDING PUT OPTIONS

Selling a put option is a bet that the stock won't go down too much. You sell someone the privilege to put the stock to you at a specific strike price. This is different from buying a put option, a bet that the stock will move down. For our strategy, we are only using the selling of put options.

We sell a put option for a particular expiration date, and we collect a premium for selling the option. Contrast this with buying a call option. With calls, we're paying for the privilege, but not the obligation, to buy the stock at a specific strike price in the future. When we sell a put option, we're selling someone the privilege of forcing us to buy the stock at the strike price if it dips.

In other words, when selling puts, you're selling them the privilege to put the stock to you at a specific strike price, on a specific expiration date. If the stock price is below your strike price at the moment of expiration, then you are obligated to buy the stock at the strike price and you are credited for the amount of the premium you received up front.

Let's say the stock is $100 on Monday, and you're selling the buyer the right to put that stock to you on Friday—a week away—for a $90 strike price. You sell a put option for $0.50 per share perhaps, and the minimum amount you can trade is one contract, which represents 100 shares. So you are selling them the right to put the stock to you on Friday at a $90 strike price for a premium of $0.50 per share. So for the hundred shares, you're collecting $50 on Monday.

If the stock is $95 on Friday, they won't put it to you for the simple reason that they don't want to buy it for $95 in the open market and sell it to you for $90, because they will lose $5 per share on the trade.

If the price is $88 on Friday, they will put it to you because they're going to buy it for $88 in the open market and put it to you for the strike price of $90, so they're going to make $2. In that case, you'll be behind $2 because you're forced to buy it for $90, and the stock's trading at $88. Now, remember you did collect a $0.50 premium on Monday. So really, your adjusted cost is not $90, but rather $89.50.

So the bet you are making when selling this put is that the stock will not fall below the strike price by expiration. It doesn't matter much if the price fluctuates during the period. Your brokerage might ask you to put up more cash in the interim, but you will really only care where the price is at expiration. If the strike price is less than the stock price at expiration, you win your bet and you keep the premium and any cash you put up.

You made your $0.50 per share. It's yours to keep. There's no further obligation.

If the price is below $90 on Friday, the stock will be put to you. You will own the stock at $90, less the premium you collected on Monday for $0.50. So you'll own it for $89.50, and this happens over the weekend after expiration date. It automatically appears in your account. Come Monday you will own 100 shares at $89.50. Is that a bad thing? Not necessarily. This is important to understand.

Let's say the stock is $100 on Monday, and it's one of your favorite stocks, and come Friday, it's down to $90, and it gets put to you. Do you mind? I'd argue that maybe you do not mind at all. If it's one of your favorite stocks, and it just had a 10 percent dip, that's not a bad deal. You're buying it at 10 percent off. Now, of course, you can say, "Yes, but it may fall further. It may fall 15 percent, or it may fall 20 percent."

That's exactly the problem. Ideally, you'd always like to buy in at the very bottom on a dip of your favorite stock. Who doesn't want to get in at the bottom? Of course, you do, but you know it's not possible. No one can pick the bottom. What I mean by that is that you would need to be a soothsayer to predict the exact moment when the bottom occurs, and we are not soothsayers. So all you can do is get in at a discount and hope you got in around the bottom.

So you're happy to get the stock at a substantial discount. If you want to be more conservative, pick a lower strike price. For example, on Monday, pick a strike price 15 percent below the current price. You'll get a bit less of a premium for the option. Instead of getting $0.50, you may only get $0.25 because you're making a more conservative bet. Also, you don't need to start the trade on Monday. You can make the trade any day before expiration. However, the premium that you collect upfront will be less as it approaches the expiration date.

Now, what happens on the following Monday after this "assignment of the stock" occurs? In my experience, more often than not, the stock price will rebound the next week. Maybe on Monday, maybe by Wednesday, maybe not till Friday, perhaps a week from Friday, but it does tend to rebound. And why is that? Well, because stocks move, and there's this phrase that stock pickers use called "reversion to the mean." What do they mean by that? They mean that stocks tend to be somewhat volatile, and they tend to come back somewhat to the course they were on.

In other words, the price often returns somewhat to where it was before it got crazy for a moment.

That is not guaranteed to be the result, but it makes sense that if a good stock takes a 15 percent dip without any earnings report to explain it, there is some reason to expect it will bounce back some.

When you sell a put expiring this Friday on your favorite stock, it might expire in the green, that is, above your strike price. You'll end up keeping the premium that you received on Monday. That's all you get; it's not much, but you got it without much risk because all you did was bet it wouldn't fall too much. Alternatively, if the stock takes an unexpected dip on Thursday or Friday, and the stock gets put to you over the weekend, now you own the stock at a substantial discount. You initially feel disappointed that your put bet didn't turn out as you had expected, but this could be a good outcome anyway!

For me, these are both pretty reasonable outcomes. I'm not nervous about either of them. I embrace them. For most weeks, I've placed perhaps ten put option positions, that is, put options that I've sold on Monday, Tuesday, or Wednesday, betting that these different stocks won't fall more than the strike price by the coming Friday expiration. And as Friday comes, they usually all expire in the money. I collect all these premiums. Maybe one stock fell more than the others on Friday for some odd reason. And all of a sudden, I own that one stock. Do I feel bad about that? No. I just bought one of my favorite stocks at a discount from what it was a few days ago. This is good. Admittedly the bet didn't come out exactly as I predicted, but the alternative is still a good result. I own a favorite stock at a hefty discount off its recent price.

I look at it this way: I like this particular company, and I am thinking of maybe buying their stock. But instead of paying the listed price on Monday for the stock, I can buy it the following Monday for perhaps 10 percent less. Such a deal!

CHOOSING PUT OPTIONS

To choose the exact put you want to sell, start by looking at the snapshot of a stock that has some volatility. Then look at the five-day chart to see the low price of the past five days. My starting assumption is that the stock will not drop much, if any, below the lowest number of the past five-day chart, unless it is going to report earnings during the week. Generally, I avoid stocks reporting earnings during the week unless I have some confidence it will be great earnings. Otherwise, I look for another stock to sell puts on.

If the stock is too staid, too conservative, and doesn't move much, that put option premium will be too low to be very meaningful. Stocks that have more action are good candidates, and there are lots of them to choose from. Tesla is a volatile stock and moves a lot, so it is a good choice to sell puts on, but choose a conservative strike price—a price that it probably will not reach. Facebook is more consistent, that is, it moves less, so it is less likely to drop below the low of the past five days. Same with Amazon, Chipotle, or Salesforce. If you choose to sell a put option on these, you do not need to be as conservative as with Tesla.

The more volatile the stock is, that is, the more it moves up and down a lot in a short time, the more you want to choose a safer strike price for your puts. And a safer strike price means a greater margin for movement. So if Tesla is $650, maybe the strike is $590, which is roughly a 10 percent drop. With a less volatile stock, you can get closer to the actual stock price. For example, if Apple is $132, you could use a strike as close as $128, a 3 percent drop, because Apple doesn't move as much.

I recommend you look at the five-day and thirty-day charts to see how low it has been and how much the stock has been moving in the past month.

The actual process of choosing the put option to sell is this:

- Look for a put option that will expire in one to two weeks.

- Check the strike price. Is it lower than any price in the previous five days? If the stock has not been that low in the past five days, I feel more confident that it will probably not drop that low in the next five days.

Do not do this during its earnings reporting week, which creates too much volatility in the price.

> > 100 < <

REAL-LIFE EXAMPLE: SELLING PUT OPTIONS

Let's look at one of my favorite stocks, Etsy (ETSY). The stock has had a good run. They reported excellent sales in January 2021, and the stock jumped from $135 to $155 in a week. That's a big jump. So it is trading for $155.

I'm going to click on "Options" and look at a put option. And you recall, we only sell put options that are a week or two out. It's a bit of a judgment to decide how much risk I want to take. There is a mathematical formula that's more exacting, and we'll talk about that later in this chapter. For now, I want to talk about using some common sense. I'm going to click on "Options," then click "All," for one week out. I see, on a Tuesday, that the stock is $155. What's the chance it's going to drop to $147 by Friday? The market's almost closed. I will be exposed to the price movement on Wednesday, Thursday, and Friday. I've got three days before the expiration of the option. What's the chance it's going to drop from $155 to $147, which is over a 5 percent drop?

It's unlikely it will drop to $147 unless it's reporting earnings in the next three days. So I check the Snapshot screen to see when the next earnings report will occur. It's months away because they just reported earnings, and that's why the stock jumped in a week. So I think there's a good likelihood the stock will not drop to $147 in a week.

Let's go two weeks out, though, and see how that option looks. The stock is $155. What's the likelihood it'll drop from $155 to $142 in the next 11 days? I don't think that is likely to happen.

I don't think it's likely to drop that much because they just reported earnings, the stock jumped, and there is obvious enthusiasm for the stock. What would cause it to turn around and drop $13 in 11 days?

This seems like a reasonably safe bet. I can get $1.29 per share by selling a put option with expiration in ten days. So I click on "Sell Open." That means I'm opening the trade. Sell open, one contract representing 100 shares at a strike of $142, expiring ten days from now. And the bid is $1.32. The ask is $1.44.

I have to look at the bid because that's what they're offering. They're bidding $1.32. So I'm going to put it in at a limit of $1.35 and see if the order fills at that price. I'm going to click on "Good for 60 Days" because it may not fill today, but it might fill tomorrow. Next, I'm going to "Preview the Order." It says I would collect $134, which is the $1.34 times 100 shares, for one option contract.

A week from Friday, I will have completed the trade, and collected $134 for betting it wouldn't drop from $155 to $142. Now, if I change that to ten contracts, for example, I would click on "Change Order." I'm going to click ten contracts instead of one contract. Now, I'm controlling 1,000 shares at the same price. I'll collect $1,346 for ten contracts.

Sounds like a reasonably safe bet? Either way, the put option will be over in a week or two, so we'll know the answer soon.

So that's selling a put option. It's a fun bet. Why? First, you don't need the stock to go up. All you need to do is have the stock not go down too much. Second, if you do get it wrong, and the worst thing happens, and the stock gets put to you, you're buying it at what appears to be a great price. So I like to think of this as a "win" either way if it's one of your favorite stocks.

It's back to this simple principle: sell puts on stocks you love and that you would like to own because there's a chance you may own them at the end of the week. And you'll own them at a nice discount to the current price. And, as we might say, any time you can get a stock you love at 10 percent off, why not? It's a terrific price. Be happy. You might be showing a loss on the position because the stock dipped so much on Friday. But in my experience, if it has an irrational dip on Friday, and it gets put to you over the weekend, there is an excellent chance that it will come back up, and you will soon be seeing green for this position.

Don't do this on a stock you don't like. Pick stocks you love. If you could get them at a discount, consider yourself lucky. Most of the big gains I made in my life have been put options that got put to me at the end of a bad market week or after a bad Friday dip. I had to buy the stock, but the next week or the next two weeks or the next month, the stock went up substantially, and I made a lot of money.

If your favorite stock is in a slow upward trend, it may have a momentary drop, or it may have a momentary spike, but there'll be a tendency for it to revert to the mean. I've seen in my experience that after a stock is put to me on a Friday, I'm behind 3 or 4% in the investment over the weekend. All of a sudden I own 100 shares (or 1,000 shares as the case may be). The stock is put to me, and by Monday, I'm behind. But within a week or two, I've made a positive 3, 4, or 5%.

Many times, after holding this new stock position for a few weeks or a month, the unrealized gain is a lot more than the premium I collected for the put option.

HOW MUCH CASH IS REQUIRED FOR PUT OPTION TRADES?

Because stocks might be put to you, if you sell put options, you must have some extra cash available to cover the cost of the stocks. It happens that the brokerage, such as E*TRADE, takes and holds a lot of your cash when you sell put options, and they hold that until Friday when the put expires. So you get it back in a week or two, but you are required to have the cash available.

E*TRADE computes the cash required for put option trades by taking the number of shares the trade represents and multiplying that usually by 20% (for some more volatile stocks, they might hold a greater percentage). In the Etsy (ETSY) example above, it represents 1,000 shares at $142. So that's about $142,000 worth of stock, and 20% of that would be $28,400. I'd need to have $28,000 in my portfolio to collect this $1,346 premium if I sell ten contracts. This is possible because I am qualified for Level 3 Options Trades.

If by chance you are not approved for Level 3 Options trading or if you are trading in your IRA, they will let you place the trade but hold the entire amount of $142,000, which would make the return on investment so low that it is not worth doing.

The amount of cash being held back can sometimes differ from one brokerage to another and from one stock to another, so you will need to ask how it works where you are investing.

Let's go back and look at it for one contract again. One contract is 100 shares. I'm controlling 100 shares at a $142 strike price. Use your calculator and multiply 100 shares times a strike price of $142 times 20%. I'm putting up to $2,840 for the privilege of collecting $134 in ten days.

It does take a bit of cash to make this trade, but this is a solid trade in my opinion. I don't think the stock is dropping from $155 to $142 in 11 days. There's no reason for that to happen. There's no earnings report coming up. Now, what if the worst thing happened, and it did drop, and by a week from this Friday, it drops to $141 and it gets put to me at $142?

My first observation is that I'm collecting $135 ($1.35 per share). E*TRADE will credit me $135, and that will lower the cost price of this stock in my portfolio from $142 down to $140.65. So I'm buying one of my favorite stocks, Etsy, which was trading at $155 that day, for $140.65. Is that a good deal? I think so! It's a great deal. The stock was $155, and someone wanted to sell it to me for $140.65? Sure, why not? I'll take that deal!

Over the weekend, if it got put to me at $142, that is not a taxable transaction. Rather that's a seamless exercising of the option into the stock (you do not do anything, it just happens automatically). So just like with calls at the expiration, with puts at the expiration, if it does get put to you, that is not a taxable transaction. It is noteworthy that you will feel a lot better about this situation if you have enough cash to afford to take the stock that is put to you. If you do not have enough cash, what will happen is that it gets put to you over the weekend, and simultaneously you receive a margin call on Monday telling you that you are short of cash to cover the entire amount. But that is okay. As mentioned earlier, you will just sell some of the position to cover the required cash.

When the market opens on Monday, if the stock you just acquired jumps back up, then you still have the margin call but have a day to settle it. You might close out part of the trade and make a profit. Or it might jump up enough that you only need to sell a small portion. Or you might sell the entire position and make a profit and get your cash back for another trade. These are very good outcomes, which are possible because you waited until expiration and looked at the situation on Monday.

If the stock does not jump up or sinks further, you will need to address the margin call by the end of the day. You could add funds, or you could sell the stock or sell another position. Now you are betting that it will rebound on Tuesday, Wednesday, or Thursday, and it often does. This is a judgment call: do you get out and take a smaller profit or a loss, or do you wait and see?

THE FORMULA FOR CALCULATING PERCENTAGE RETURN ON A PUT OPTION TRADE

Let's put a finer point on the discussion by coming up with the actual percentage return for a put option. Calculating the percentage return of a put option trade will help determine if the trade is worth making.

Here is the formula:

(Total premium collected) ÷ (Capital required) × (Number of periods in a year) = (Annualized rate of return)

Let's use the Facebook example of selling a put option and collecting a premium of $1.13 per share with a strike price of $237. Since one option contract is for 100 shares, that means the total premium you collect is $113.

A premium of $113, divided by capital required, multiplied by 52 (if the option expires in one week) equals the annualized rate of return. If it expires in two weeks, you would multiply by 26.

In the case of E*TRADE, the capital required is usually 20% or $4,740 ($237 strike price × 100 shares = $23,700, × 20%), which is held by E*TRADE for the week you are making this trade.

I do a quick calculation to see the annual percentage return on this weekly trade by taking the $1.13 and dividing it by the money required to make the trade. Then I multiply that by 52 since there are 52 weeks in a year. To find out the annualized return on this trade, we start with your total option premium, $113 (100 × $1.13), then divide that by $4,740 ($237 × 100 × 20%), then multiply it by 52 weeks in a year, and the grand total equals 1.24, or a 124% annualized return on your investment. That is fantastic!

That is the calculation if you make the trade on a Monday. If you did it on a Wednesday, you calculate it multiplying by 182 (365 divided by 2), since the money is only invested for two days, Wednesday afternoon until Friday afternoon. My objective is to get an annualized return of 100% or better.

To be more exact, note that the trade is made on a Monday, and you get the cash that E*TRADE is holding returned to you by the next Saturday. E*TRADE holds your cash for five days. A year (365 days), divided by 5, is really 73 periods in a year. If I do the calculation again using 73 instead of 52, it looks like this: $113 divided by $4,740, multiplied by 73, which is an annualized rate of return of 174%. Fantastic.

I use 52 just because it is convenient. Regardless, you are getting an annualized rate of return of about 124–174% return. Remember, this is a rate of return for the week. You only get that for the full year if you did this every single period of the year repeatedly—which we are not.

This might seem complicated at first, but it isn't really. Just take the number of shares, multiplied by the premium, then divided by the capital required, and multiplied by 52 (if it expires in a week) to get the annualized return.

I used 52 in this example because the contract expires in a week, and there are 52 weeks in a year. If you made a contract that is two weeks out, you would multiply by 26 instead. If the contract expired in ten days, you would multiply by 36.5 (365 days in a year divided by ten).

After you do the calculation, you can decide if you want to make the trade. If the annualized rate of return on the trade is below 50 percent, you might decide to pass on it.

WHEN DO PUTS NOT WORK WELL?

I've learned through experience not to sell put options when the market is continually going down, such as what we saw in early February to mid-March 2020. Every week the averages seemed to be going lower and dragging everything down with them. The problem with selling puts then was that we would be betting that the stock would not go down too much by Friday, but it did go down further. And that pattern repeated for about six weeks in a row.

So, the takeaway is this: When the markets are in retreat, when things seem negative and going down every week, take a break from selling puts. Just sit back and wait for things to turn around. You can nibble in with long-dated calls, averaging in slowly, but do not sell puts until the sun comes out and the averages start climbing again, or at least have stabilized. Selling puts is a strategy that works best in a market that is fairly stable, and not going down all the time.

Or, it works well with a particular stock that you judge is in a fairly stable or upward pattern. For example, Boeing (BA) had a recent high in June 2021 of $250 but then lost 20% and dropped to $205 on July 19, 2021. In a month, it dropped 20%, on various pieces of news that were not positive, such as the Delta variant of the COVID-19 virus, with the expected dampening of economic recovery, as well as a few safety checks from the FAA that gave investors a cautious note.

This is a good example of how following the news regularly gives you confidence that you can buy into a stock and expect it to move upward because you've interpreted the news to be only a momentary event.

In this case, the fact that there have been a few FAA comments that dinged the stock in the past week is, to me, only a momentary event. The news reported that it should be cleared up in two or three weeks. It is not news that should change the general upward trajectory of the stock.

Compared to a mere momentary event, the distinction between trend changes is important, and something you get from following the news. See Pro Trading Tip #9 in the bonus section of this book.

Your annualized rate of return is a useful measurement to ensure that the put option transaction gives you a reasonable rate of return, or at least one that meets your goals. I want to see an annualized return on the investment that is roughly a 100% annualized return.

Sometimes I take a lower return if it seems like a really safe (conservative) bet.

You take the amount of cash that your brokerage holds to complete the trade; at E*TRADE, this is usually 20% of the stock value. So if it is ten contracts at a strike price of $207.50, that would be $41,500 held until the expiration of the option ($207.5 × 1,000 shares × 20%).

Then, take the premium that you received for selling the put, which in this case turned out to be $1.30 per share, multiplied times 1,000 shares (ten contracts), or $1,300, and divide that by the amount of cash held, $41,500, and then multiply that by the period you are holding it.

In this example, the option expires in 9 days, so I divide 365 days by nine and get about 40 periods in a year—we are computing an annualized return, so we need to convert the 9-day return to a year's return.

So, here is the final computation:

$1,300 divided by $41,500 multiplied by 40, which is 1.25, or a return of 125% on an annualized basis.

BOEING (BA)

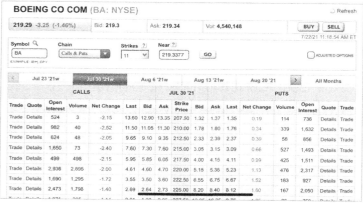

BOEING CO COM (BA: NYSE) ↻ Refresh

| 219.29 -3.25 (-1.46%) | Bid: 219.3 | Ask: 219.34 | Vol: 4,540,148 | BUY | SELL |

7/22/21 11:18:54 AM ET

| Symbol 🔍 | Chain | Strikes ? | Near ? | | |
| BA | Calls & Puts ▾ | 11 ▾ | 219.3377 | GO | ☐ ADJUSTED OPTIONS |

EXAMPLE: IBM, SPY

| < | Jul 23 '21w | Jul 30 '21w | Aug 6 '21w | Aug 13 '21w | Aug 20 '21 | > | All Months |

CALLS						JUL 30 '21				PUTS				
Trade	Quote	Open Interest	Volume	Net Change	Last	Bid	Ask	Strike Price	Bid	Ask	Last	Net Change	Volume	Open Interest	Quote	Trade
Trade	Details	524	3	-2.15	13.60	12.90	13.35	207.50	1.32	1.37	1.35	0.19	114	736	Details	Trade
Trade	Details	982	40	-2.52	11.50	11.05	11.30	210.00	1.78	1.80	1.76	0.34	339	1,632	Details	Trade
Trade	Details	624	48	-2.05	9.65	9.10	9.35	212.50	2.33	2.39	2.37	0.39	58	856	Details	Trade
Trade	Details	1,650	73	-2.40	7.60	7.30	7.60	215.00	3.05	3.15	3.09	0.66	527	1,493	Details	Trade
Trade	Details	499	498	-2.15	5.95	5.85	6.05	217.50	4.00	4.15	4.11	0.99	425	1,511	Details	Trade
Trade	Details	2,936	2,695	-2.00	4.61	4.60	4.70	220.00	5.15	5.35	5.23	1.13	476	2,317	Details	Trade
Trade	Details	1,690	1,295	-1.72	3.55	3.50	3.60	222.50	6.55	6.75	6.67	1.52	183	927	Details	Trade
Trade	Details	2,473	1,798	-1.40	2.69	2.64	2.73	225.00	8.20	8.40	8.12	1.60	167	2,050	Details	Trade

8:11 📶 5G 🔋 🔒 us.etrade.com

Preview Order

The Sharper Fund

NYSE ↻ Refresh quote
BA BOEING CO COM

Last Price x Size / Exch ⓘ
219.64 x 239ᴷ -2.9000 (-1.30%)

Bid x size
219.56 x 300ᴷ

Ask x size
219.63 x 200ᴴ

Volume
4.00M

Action	Quantity	Description	Bid x
Sell Open	10	BA Jul 30 '21 $207.50 Put	$1.27

Price type	Price	Duration
Market	MKT	Good for Day

> View impact to purchasing power

Estimated commission **$3.00**
Estimated proceeds **$1,266.84**

Place order

Change order

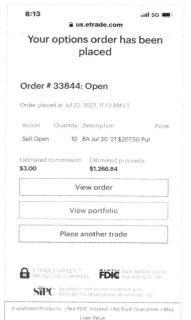

8:13 📶 5G 🔋 🔒 us.etrade.com

Your options order has been placed

Order # 33844: Open

Order placed at Jul 22, 2021, 11:13 AM ET

Action	Quantity	Description	Price
Sell Open	10	BA Jul 30 '21 $207.50 Put	

Estimated commission Estimated proceeds
$3.00 **$1,266.84**

View order

View portfolio

Place another trade

🔒 E*TRADE COMPLETE™ PROTECTION GUARANTEE FDIC Member · Bank deposits insured to at least $250,000

SIPC Securities in your account protected up to $500,000. For details please see www.sipc.org

Investment Products: · Not FDIC Insured · No Bank Guarantee · May Lose Value

PLUG POWER (PLUG)

Plug Power, a supplier of hydrogen fuel systems, is an interesting stock because it has been so volatile, with large moves up and down. As of August 17, 2021, the stock is about $26. It had a low of $7.07 on July 31, 2020, and a high of $75.49 on January 26, 2021.

It is very rare to see a stock go up by a factor of ten in just six months and then retreat to $26 by August, 2021.

I considered selling put options on it in July, 2021, because it has already fallen from its high, and had been fairly stable since May 2021, which tells me that it is probably not going back to its lows.

When I looked at the put options for July 30, 2021, I saw a premium offered of about $0.27, at a strike price of $25. So I will either collect the premium, and the trade will be over in a week, or I will have the stock put to me at $25 less the $0.27, or $24.73. That seems like a reasonable risk, given that the stock has been stable and might even start climbing back up to its high, which occurred just six months ago.

I look at the annualized rate of return, which we compute as in the Boeing example. For 50 contracts, or 5,000 shares, with a premium of .27, it is $1,350 collected upfront, and we divide that by the cash held (5,000 × $25 × 20%), which is $25,000. So, $1,350 divided by $25,000 is .054, and then I multiply that by 52 since I am holding it for a week, and that equals 2.8, or a 280% annualized rate of return. This is an excellent percentage return, so I like this trade!

Here are some screenshots of the actual trade:

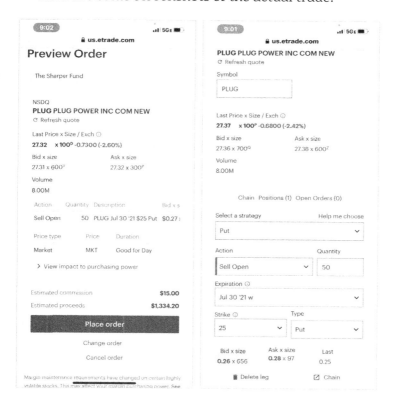

ZOOM (ZM) IN MARCH OF 2021

Let me share an example of a put trade that went wrong. This happens now and then, and is an unusual, unexpected fluke, but that is part of trading in the market. You want to think that everything in the market is rational, but it isn't, so we just live with it being disappointing now and then.

Remember, the total of your winnings and your losses is your net result, and hopefully that adds up to be positive. Every trade will not be a winner. And the occasional loss is part of the game.

I had an unfortunate and completely unforeseeable result the week of March 1, 2021. Zoom, the video conferencing company, reported great earnings on March 1, and the stock climbed in the after-hours trading, reflecting this great report. It eventually got to a high the next morning of $429, up about $30. I sold puts for the coming Friday, four days away, with a strike price of $407, meaning I'm betting the stock won't fall below $407. That seemed like a reasonable margin for error. Who would think the stock would drop from $429 to $407, or over 5%, when it just reported these great earnings and the stock was moving up on the news? This is a very safe situation because there is no logic for why the stock would retreat and go down, and if it did, this would be a good entry point at $407, right?

Usually, I want to have a strike price of about 8–12% below the current price, so this was short of that, but they had just reported earnings, and the stock popped, which gave me confidence that the stock price would not retreat in the next day or two. However, I did violate my rule, which turned out to be a mistake, though the stock price action was unexpected and unpredictable.

So this turned out to be an example of where I made a mistake, and one which has gotten me into trouble before, which is that I felt so confident in this situation that I doubled my bet, and ended up with 200 put option contracts sold for Friday.

Much to my surprise, the very next day the stock dropped to $390, which was below my strike price, and that would result at the end of the week, with 20,000 shares being put to me, with a market value of over $7 million. Rather than take the stock and put out that much money, and have an outsized investment with an unrealized loss showing, I decided to close out the position and take a $200,000 loss.

Then I attempted to recover my loss by selling another 200 put options, this time with a strike price of $365. That seemed like a really safe bet, because the stock was at $429 a couple of days before, and it somehow dropped to $390. Certainly, I could have confidence it would not drop below $365, right? Given that the company just reported great earnings, and given that the stock popped to $429 the next day, and given that the stock market, in general, was steady, it seemed like a safe bet that the stock was not going to drop to $365—right?

Wrong! It is a mystery to me, but somehow it closed out that Friday at $337, and I had a new unrealized loss of $600,000! Unbelievable! I had lost almost $1 million in a week selling what looked like "safe" puts on Zoom. And the crazy thing is that it reported earnings early in the week that were a blowout, yet by Friday, the stock dropped 100 points or about 25 percent! This is bizarre and makes no sense. Normally a stock that reports superb earnings does not drop 25 percent in a week. It is really unheard of, but it happened.

You will probably never see a situation like this, and I certainly hope I never see one again. If there is any lesson to be learned, it is not to place too large a bet on any one position, because strange things do happen. I made this mistake because I got overconfident that a particular bet looked like a sure thing. And then, I was surprised that it went against me. Lesson learned repeatedly: Do not place too big a bet, no matter how confident you are. There is a chance it will not work out the way you expect!

HOLDING POSITIONS

Sometimes it happens that I have a large stock position put to me on a Saturday because I sold puts that expired, and the stock dropped below my strike price on that last Friday. That happens with some frequency. Now comes Monday. I now own 5,000 shares of some favorite companies because they got put to me over the weekend. Remember, each option contract is 100 shares, so if 50 contracts were put to me, that is a 5,000-share position put to me.

If you had sold one put contract during the week, that would be 100 shares, and if it gets put to you on Saturday because the stock dropped 15 percent, then you would own 100 shares of this favorite stock, and you bought it at a nice discount. Even though your put option did not turn out as you predicted, this is a good result!

Remember, when you sell put options, you are collecting an option premium upfront, say $0.50 per share. If you sell 50 put option contracts, you collect (50 × 100 × $0.50), or $2,500. There are 100 shares represented per contract, so if it is an option premium of $0.50 per share, for 50 contracts, which represents 5,000 shares, at $0.50 each, that is $2,500 that you collect up front.

When the option expires in a week, one of two things happens. It could expire "in the money," which means you keep the $2,500, and the trade is over and done. Or, it could "end in the red" because the stock price at expiration is below the option strike price. Then, the stock will be put to you, and you will own shares of this stock at the strike price, less the credit for the initial $0.50.

It might be a lot of money. For example, if it were Amazon, five contracts, or 500 shares, would be about $1,500,000—over 1.5 million dollars! Such a large amount of cash tied up in stock is not helping our strategy, especially when I believe it is much more efficient to buy call options rather than the stock. So in this situation, I would consider selling all 500 shares. If I want to hold the position, I would consider replacing it by buying five contracts of two-year-out call options.

Another way to look at selling put options on a weekly or bi-weekly basis is you want to be emotionally invested in your investments. And by that, I mean you really want to like the company and want to own the stock. I had an example recently.

There was a crazy stock called Fubo TV, FUBO is the symbol. It's a soccer league betting site, soccer as in football. And I don't follow betting stocks. I don't like sports betting stocks. They just don't appeal to me. Maybe because I don't personally use them, I don't know which are the best ones. But this stock had performed really well for the past month and had been in the news.

So I took a flyer. The stock was around $50. I sold a put, betting it would not go to $25 in two weeks. I never thought it would go from $50 to $25 in two weeks in my wildest imagination. That seemed like a really safe bet, right?

As it turns out, the stock did drop to $23 before the expiration date, and I was getting worried that it would get put to me, and it is not a stock that I wanted to own. I violated my rule to only sell puts on stocks that I am comfortable owning. It was not looking good, but as it turned out, by the expiration date the stock was above $25, and I kept my option premium, and the trade was over. Thank goodness! If you had asked me if I ever wanted to buy that stock, I would say no.

LONG-DATED PUTS

People often ask, "Why not sell longer-dated puts?" The premium's a lot higher. If you sell a put for this Friday, you might collect $0.25 to $0.50 a share. If you sell a put for the next Friday, two weeks out, you might collect $0.50 to $1 a share. But if you sell a put six months out, you might collect $3 to $5.

So why not sell puts six months out? Well, I tried that one year, and I found that you can lose a lot of money selling long-dated puts because when you sell, the word "sell" is the clue. If you sell something in the stock market, someday you'll have to buy it back, and buying something back at a price that could go to the sky means your losses are unlimited. As a result, I stick to my rule that I only sell put options that are out for a maximum of two weeks. If the stock is one you love, and you really want to sell puts on it, and it only has monthly options, then you wait for a week or so until the expiration is two weeks out.

This may be too strict a rule, but I stick to it in order to prevent a large unexpected loss. There are plenty of gains to be had, and plenty of losses to be had, without opening ourselves to the risk of puts that are too far out.

KEY POINTS FROM CHAPTER 6

1. To choose the exact put to sell, start by looking at the snapshot of a stock with some volatility. If the stock is too staid, too conservative, and doesn't move much, that put option premium will be too low. Stocks that have more action are better candidates.

2. You must have cash available to sell put options to cover the cost of the stocks. The brokerage will take and hold a lot of your cash when you sell put options—about 20% of the value of the stock should it get put to you. They hold that until

> > 122 < <

Friday when the put expires, and return it to your account at expiration if you are in the money.

3. Formula to calculate a put return: (total premium collected) divided by (capital required) multiplied by (number of periods in a year) equals the (annualized rate of return).

4. When you sell put options, you are collecting an option premium up front, and exposing yourself to the risk of unlimited loss.

5. Only sell put options that are for a maximum of two weeks out, to help prevent the possibility of a large, unexpected loss.

6. When the markets are in retreat and when things seem to be negative and going down every week, take a break from selling puts.

CHAPTER 7

STRATEGIES FOR SUCCESS

N ow that we've learned about the different kinds of trades we'll be making, here are some strategies you can use to level up your trading and reach that 30–50% benchmark we're aiming for with *The Sharper Investor Winning Formula.*

REMEMBER: BUY LOW, SELL HIGH

The secret to making this or any stock buying system work is one simple phrase: "buy low, sell high." We want to buy a stock or option at a lower price than we eventually sell it at. Sounds pretty obvious, doesn't it? Yet, so many people don't do it that way. Instead, they buy into a position. Then the market takes a downward turn; it starts to crash. Guess what they say to themselves?

"I'd better sell out now while there's still something left." So they have bought high, and now they're considering selling low. Well, that's the opposite of what you want to do.

You want to wait until the market, or your favorite stocks, have a big dip, which it does with some regularity, and then buy call options at a low price, and hold until they eventually go up some, and then you can either let them roll into the stock at expiration, or you can sell for a profit. You've bought low and you're going to sell high. This is so simple and yet it's actually quite difficult to do in practice. Why? Because our emotions get hold of us and we get scared; we sell at the low because we fear losing everything.

I've seen it again and again with my friends. We talk about buying into a dip, but when it comes, they get discouraged and don't feel comfortable nibbling in. It is a typical reaction that when the market is really down, you do not feel like buying. I completely understand because your emotions tell you to wait and watch. But my experience is that you must force yourself to nibble in when prices drop more than 20 percent. Just do it slowly and average in, and have confidence that it will be a good decision! And remember, you are not going all in. Instead, you are putting in a small portion and waiting till another day or another week to put in some more. You are averaging in.

RISK EQUALS REWARD

Even with my simple method, you could still lose money. That's always a risk, and let's not forget the simple cliche, "risk equals reward." What do we mean by that? Simply that, in general, the more risk you take, the greater the reward, and the less risk you take, the less reward. When you go to your bank, or savings and loan, and take out a CD (certificate of deposit), and get paid 1 percent or less, you have a lot of safety, but you don't have much return. On the other hand, we are taking more risk, but I think we will manage it well so that we avoid a disaster.

How are we managing risk? Remember, we only use two strategies: we sell put options a week or two weeks out, and we are buying call options two years out.

Selling puts one or two weeks out is riskier than buying a call option two years out. Why are calls less risky in terms of potential loss? Because when you buy the call, that is the total amount you can lose. You have capped your potential loss by the amount you paid for the call.

When you sell a put, if it by chance goes against you, in theory, your potential loss is unlimited because you must buy it back at some point, and that is potentially a number that causes a very big loss. That is why I limit our put selling to just one, or at most two weeks, until expiration. That has the effect of keeping any possible loss to a minimum because the time period is so short that your exposure is limited.

When you buy call options, you are limiting your loss to the price you pay that day. If you put $1,000 into it, that's all you can lose. And the keyword is the word "buy." When you are buying something, that's all you can lose.

When you sell something, the keyword is "sell." That is a signal to warn you that your loss is potentially unlimited if you are selling something. So to repeat, if your first part of the trade is to buy, your loss is limited. If the first part of your trade is to sell, your loss is unlimited.

I acknowledge that the potential loss on a put option is unlimited, and the potential loss on a call option is limited to what you paid up front. However, I'd also point out that in one respect the put is a more conservative bet than the call: because when you sell the put, you are betting that it will not fall too much by Friday. Compare that to buying a call, which requires that the underlying stock go up for you to avoid losing your investment.

So in that sense, the put is a safer bet. It only requires the stock not to drop too much. The call requires the stock to go up. However, this analysis is further complicated by the fact that buying a call option that is two years out requires very little cash in comparison to the put option, which requires a lot of cash up front.

WHICH IS BETTER?
SELLING WEEKLY PUT OPTIONS OR
BUYING LONG-DATED CALL OPTIONS?

They're definitely very different.

My experience has been that selling put options a week or two out can be a relatively safe bet. Most weeks I'll place maybe 10 or 20 different bets, that is, individual put sell positions. I'm using the word "bet," though really that's not what E*TRADE would call it. They'd call it an investment. I'd call it a bet.

Typically 19 out of the 20 bets, or sold put options, will expire in the money, meaning I keep the put option premium and the trade is over. Maybe for one or two out of 20, I will have bet the wrong way. In other words, the stock fell too much by Friday below my strike price. It gets put to me, and now I own the stock.

Some of my best investments ever have been stocks that got put to me, and I've held the stock. What usually happens is the stock rebounds the following week or the following two weeks, and I'm back in the green again. The reason for this is when a stock drops an unusually large amount on a Friday, it is a somewhat irrational drop.

> > 129 < <

In other words, it is a bit of an anomaly. That is the reason that it often rebounds the next week. The drop on the previous Friday was not logical. Then the stock returns to a more normal price. Why did it have that irrational drop on Friday? In my experience, the professional big traders sometimes do not want to hold positions over a weekend, so they close out on their position on Friday. If there are not many buyers, the stock drops a larger amount than would seem rational.

With long-dated call options, as a contrast to puts, you have the opportunity to make the big money, and you do it with a lot less cash. Buying call options two years out doesn't take nearly as much money as buying the stock, and it takes less money than selling the put.

When you buy long-dated call options, you pay for it all in advance, but it's not a very high premium. It's actually a fairly inexpensive premium compared to the puts. So you're not investing a lot of money. If the stock goes up over the next six months, a year, or two years, you will make a lot more money with calls than puts.

My biggest gains by far have been from buying long-dated call options. The problem is it only works if the stock goes up. If the stock goes down, or stays the same, those long-dated call options are not going to make you any money. Contrast that with selling puts. That is just simply a bet that the stock won't go down too much by

Friday. You won't make as much money, but it's relatively safe. We're back to "risk equals reward."

I do both. I trade by selling put options one week out or two weeks out, and I'm regularly making money. Compare it to the baseball analogy. It's like hitting singles every week. I'm just banging out these singles. They're only singles. They're not doubles. They're not triples. They're singles. Buying call options two years out could be a home run, sometimes many times over. That's where the big money is. That's where the home runs are. But it's a different bet. You're betting the stock will go up. Now we can tweak this, and make it work better for us by using one simple technique.

WAIT FOR THE DIP

I want to emphasize how important it is to take advantage of dips. Let's look at January 4, 2021, when the market had a big drop. The Nasdaq was down over 250 points. The Dow Jones was down 600 points. And what should you think when the market has a big drop like that? You should think this is a good day to nibble in buying long-dated calls, following our formula that we want to buy low and sell high. And on a day when the market has tanked, we have a better opportunity to buy low.

Let's contrast that with the opposite. The markets had a great day and you say to yourself, "Wow, this market is booming. I should buy some long-dated calls because this market is going up." Well, that's not a good approach because you want to buy low and sell high.

The dips that are mentioned above turned out to be good short-term buys but were eclipsed by the drop during the week of March 1, 2021. That week saw a lot of technology stocks drop by 20 percent or even 30 percent, and this was just within the week!

Such dramatic moves in one week are scary. It is always a stomach-churning experience to see your favorite stock positions tumble in value. It was across the board, hitting all the high-tech leaders that had propelled the market higher in the previous year.

What caused this drop? News articles seem to suggest that a rise in interest rates was going to spell trouble for these high valuation stock leaders. I wonder about that, as it certainly does not make any sense that a slight rise in interest rates would cause people to buy less pizza from Domino's, or buy less Mexican food from Chipotle, or do less video conferencing with Zoom, or decide not to buy an Apple product.

What to do during this brutal drop? My strategy is to nibble in and buy call options that are two years out on my favorite stocks. I'm avoiding selling puts when the market is taking big lurches downward because they can run up a significant loss quickly, as described in Chapter 6 with my Zoom debacle.

AVERAGING IN

When a bunch of the very finest stocks like Apple, Amazon, Tesla, Nvidia, and Restoration Hardware fall dramatically in a week by as much as 20 percent or more, my thinking is to buy some long-dated calls and spread them out so that you are nibbling in, or averaging in.

Averaging in is one of the basic concepts that all savvy investors use, and you should use it too.

It just simply means buy a little bit today and wait. Maybe in a few days, or in a week, if you like it, especially if it's gone down some more, buy a little more. The worst that can happen is it turns around and runs up, in which case you're not going to buy any more at a lower price. But so what? There'll be other opportunities. Averaging in with long-dated calls when the markets are heading down can be a very profitable approach.

The best plan for averaging in is to spread your planned investment into four or five tranches or lots. Buy in today with 25 percent of your planned investment. Then wait, maybe a week, maybe a month, and then buy in another 25 percent. Then wait another two weeks, or even a month, and put another 25 percent to work. Finally, after another two weeks or a month, put the last 25 percent to work. This is intelligently averaging in. This is so much better than buying in all at once.

It is challenging to hit the exact bottom—virtually impossible—so what we are doing is bracketing the bottom, and we started investing when we saw a 20 to 30 percent drop in the stock price.

Of course, to do this, you need to have some cash left to invest. That is always something you need to keep an eye on. Jim Cramer likes to call it "keeping some powder dry," or in other words, always have some cash available to buy long-dated calls if the market has a significant dip.

THE BIG DROP—AND OPPORTUNITY— IN MARCH 2020

Let's review what happened in 2020 that made my portfolio jump 261% by the end of the year.

For me, 2020 was a year of amazing opportunities, but 2020 was unusual because the markets started off fairly strong. January was okay. But by February and March, the markets were heading down in reaction to the spread of the COVID-19 virus. I recall that on the worst day, which occurred around March 23rd, the difference between the peak in late January and the bottom on March 23rd was a 30% drop. That's pretty huge.

You don't usually see a market drop 30% and certainly not in six weeks. What do we think of this? Well, one thought that occurred to me is that the coronavirus pandemic caused this. This is a situation that is probably not going to last forever. Eventually, life will probably return to normal, even though it may take a year or more.

Could we start buying long-dated calls at the bottom and make a lot of money? We could. The only problem is we don't really know where the bottom is, because no one ever accurately knows where the bottom is. What you can do is start nibbling in, or averaging in, and you'll buy some before the bottom, and you'll buy some at the bottom, and you'll buy some after the bottom. When do you start? Well, my guess was, if it's dropped 30% from top to bottom by March 23rd, which is probably about 20 percent from January 1st, that's a pretty big drop. In historic terms, you're getting near the bottom any time you see a 20–30% drop. So, it is smart to start averaging in.

I started buying some calls of my favorite stocks, long-dated calls. I focused on my favorite stocks—Amazon, Tesla, Apple, and Restoration Hardware—and on ones that benefited from the stay-at-home trend, such as Zoom, Chipotle, and Domino's Pizza. I averaged into these long-dated calls, and started at the beginning of March, figuring since the market had dropped 20–30%, it was a good time to start. And long-dated calls don't cost much because they're two years out.

You'll see it's not much money compared to buying the stock. It's typically about 15–18% of the strike price.

You're putting up 18% of the strike price for the right to control the same number of shares. And we're just slowly averaging in. They're not making any money in the first week. In fact, the market drops further. Then you keep averaging in some more. We're by accident getting into some of these stocks at the bottom which occurred about March 23. Then, I was still slowly nibbling in, after the bottom. Now, we're off the bottom a little bit.

The market goes up and down, but it's coming back up a little bit, and I'm still nibbling in. All of this adds up to a lot of call positions of my favorite stocks. And by August and September, they had dramatically gained in value. And because I bought long-dated calls instead of buying the stock, I've got a lot of leverage working in my favor. That's why, in the end, the year was really good.

CONTROLLING SCARY EMOTIONS DURING A MARKET CORRECTION

One of the hardest things to control is your emotions. Believe me, when the stock market has gone down 20 or 30%, you don't feel like buying anything. You're sick with worry. I'm sort of joking, but it's true. I don't know a single investor who's ever felt comfortable when their portfolios dropped 20 or 30%.

You have to force yourself to buy. If you want to be a Sharper Investor, you've got to force yourself to nibble in, to average in, buy a little bit, maybe not every day, but maybe every third day, or every week. You eventually will buy some before the bottom, you'll buy some at the bottom, and you'll buy some after the bottom. When you put that all together, you'll have a terrific investment. And that worked for me in 2020 and turned into a 261% gain for the year, which was exceptionally good.

Be disciplined! When I say be disciplined, I mean to stick to a few rules that make sense.

INVEST IN STOCKS THAT YOU REALLY BELIEVE IN

Don't buy calls or sell puts on stocks that you don't want to own. In other words, know the company's concept, try the product or read about it, think about it or do some research, so you're comfortable with owning that stock. Experience is a harsh teacher. I started investing when I was in my twenties, and like most young investors, I had this belief that I could look at the trends and look at the stock movements and guess where it might go tomorrow. So that's what I did.

Back in those days, there weren't even online stocks. There was just the printed paper. There were just the printed quotes every day, like in the *Wall Street Journal*, and they'd print the stock prices. I'd look at them and I'd go, "Oh, this stock has gone up half a point today."

Then, I'd look the next day. "Oh, it's gone up half a point again. I bet it'll go up again tomorrow." A lot of people do that. They just look at the flow of the numbers and guess which way they think it's going to go.

Honestly, I think that's like playing roulette in Las Vegas. I don't think there's anything to it other than luck. And we don't want to invest in luck. We want to invest with intelligence. What I've learned after all this is that a simple system like selling puts one week out, or buying long-dated calls on the right companies, is going to tilt the odds in our favor, unlike being in Las Vegas.

You know the casino house is going to have an edge. Somehow the house is going to take 1 percent or something of everything. On average, you're not going to win. You might get lucky and have a good hand. That's why people gamble. But here with the stocks, we're trying not to gamble. We're not trying to just be lucky. We're trying to pick a stock that's going to do well over the next two years. And we're going to do that by reading and following the Peter Lynch approach. Peter Lynch wrote about buying stocks that you love and have personal experience with—know the product; love the company.

MOMENTUM IS YOUR FRIEND, OR MAYBE NOT

Let's talk about momentum in stocks. This is an important factor because today many funds tend to be computer-driven. There are a lot fewer individual stock investors than there were 20 years ago, and a lot more fund, or ETF, computer-driven investors. As a result of this change, once the momentum, or movement, of the stock price trend gets going in a certain direction, it tends to keep going in that direction. In other words, if a stock is going up, it often tends to keep going up. And if it starts going down, it often tends to keep going down.

Now, I like to be a bit of a contrarian, meaning that I like to bet sometimes the other way. So when I see a stock has gone down too much because of momentum, I like to initiate a bet that it's going to turn around. And conversely, if it keeps going up too long, I might want to initiate a bet that it won't keep going up, because nothing ever goes in the same direction forever. It is true that momentum is a real effect, but it's also true that you will always see reversals if you look at any chart.

So what does that mean for us? How do we invest with that knowledge? Well, let's say the market is having a bad day. The Dow Jones Industrial Average is showing a negative number for the day, so is the S&P, so is the Nasdaq. It's a bad day in the market and yet your particular favorite stock happens to have gone up that day. Well, that's a good sign. A stock that can go green—that can go up on a down day—is a strong sign of strength for that stock. Taking the other side for a moment: the market goes up, all three averages are green; the markets are going up and your stock is red. It's going down on an up day. This is not a good sign.

This happened to me recently with a stock I invested in called Norton LifeLock. I initiated a long-call position two years out. The markets have done nothing but go up, all my favorite stocks have gone up, and I'm definitely better off than I was two weeks ago. And what has LifeLock done? It's gone down almost every day. So I decided to bite the bullet, sell it, and take the loss. That is a bad sign when the markets are going up and your favorite stock is going down. Generally, if you have a position in your portfolio that is performing poorly when the averages are heading up, consider taking that as a sign that you should get out of the position, even at a loss.

LET'S TALK ABOUT INCOME TAXES AGAIN

Taxes are such an important consideration, so I want to spend a few more moments on this. Of course, it depends on what kind of account you're trading in. If your account is taxable, like my main trading account, then you have the same problem as I do—what I have left after taxes is really what counts. There are short-term realized gains, and long-term realized gains, and my goal is to avoid realizing these gains so as to avoid taxes when legally possible.

Let's use a quick example. Let's say you buy a stock for $30, it goes to $100, and you've got $70 of gains. In California or New York, short-term gains are taxed at about 50 percent. Long-term gains are taxed at about 37 percent. Let's assume for a moment that you have short-term gains, Uncle Sam takes $35, or 50% of the $70. Now you're left with $65, not $100 ($30 you started with, plus $35 of gain after-tax). So for me in a taxable account, I always prefer to let the gains continue unrealized if possible. I don't close out the position. I'd rather have $100 worth of stock than $65 worth of cash. Now, in a non-taxable account like an IRA, there are no income taxes until later. So you don't have to worry about it for years. You can just buy or sell as you wish and not worry about the taxes. It depends on what kind of account you're trading in, and you should know this and monitor the tax consequences.

The stock market creates different taxes when you have realized short-term gains and long-term gains, and the determining point is the word "realized." And what do I mean by realized? I mean you closed out the transaction. Either you sold it at the beginning and now you're buying it back, or you bought it at the beginning and now you're selling it to close out the transaction. It doesn't matter in which order you do it in; what matters is that there are two parts to it, a buy and a sell.

That creates a realized transaction. And we want to manage this carefully because our net cash to invest, our net assets, and our net portfolio will always be net of taxes. The taxes may not be due for a quarter or the end of the calendar year, but in the end, it's going to be net of taxes.

If I've got a $20 option and that turns into $100, so now I have a profit of $80, and it's in my portfolio. I've got $100 right there in the portfolio, but if I cashed it out, if I realized the transaction by selling it for $100, I would be taxed on the gain of $80, and in California or New York, at roughly 50 percent state and federal, 50 percent of $80 is $40.

Now $40 goes in taxes, and I've got $40 of gain left. I add that to the $20 I started with, and I've got $60. Well, $60 is not $100. A moment ago in this conversation, I had $100 because I started with $20; I bought an option, it went to $100, and I've got $100 of assets in my portfolio. If I realize the gain by closing it out, I'm going to pay tax on that $80 of gain at roughly 50 percent; so in New York or California, that would be a $40 of tax on the $80. So now I've got $60, the original $20 plus the $40 leftover after-tax equals $60. I have a choice. Do I want to have $60, admittedly of cash, or do I want to have $100 in the portfolio? Usually, I prefer the $100 in the portfolio.

You've got to think about your own needs and your approach, but I'll tell you my approach: I'd rather have $100 in my portfolio and look at it every day and see $100. I don't need the $60 in cash right now anyway. If you need it for a car, then you've got to take the gain and pay the tax. But if you don't need it, let it ride because you've got $100. My portfolio has accumulated all varieties. I've got some losses that I've realized. I've got some small gains that I've realized. I've got some bigger gains. I've got some even bigger gains that I usually never realize; I just let them run. Some of them are millions of dollars because I've just let the gains run. I don't want to pay the tax. But watching the tax consequences of every situation is very important.

The only decision you have to make is if you have gains, do you want to close out the transaction and pay tax? If you have a loss, do you want to close out the transaction and take the loss? I look at everything all the time, but starting around October, because every tax year ends on a calendar basis, I start looking at my losses and gains for the year.

If I have a net gain, I try to take other losses to match against it. If I can reduce those gains down to zero by taking other losses to offset the gains, then perhaps I can reduce the net total gains number to zero, and then there's no tax due at the end of the year. I may have hundreds of thousands of dollars of gains that are unrealized because I haven't closed out those other transactions, but that's fine. The IRS is only looking at my realized—closed out—gains.

Since the only thing that's taxable is the realized gain where I've closed out the positions, I want to harvest my tax losses. In other words, I want to take these losses by the end of the calendar year. On a platform like E*TRADE or TD Ameritrade, you can click a tab that'll show your realized gains in total for the year to date, and you want to manage that down to zero. Now, if you end up with a loss for the full year, you can carry that forward forever, to the next year and beyond. So what we want to do is sell some of these positions, realize the loss, and reinvest the money in another similar but different position. Similarly, you think it has just as good a chance of going up as the position you are closing out—different in that it is not exactly the same stock or the same option. However, each different option month and the call strike price is considered different enough.

Why does it need to be different? There is a rule, called the wash sale tax, that does not allow you to use the loss for tax purposes unless the new position has a different CUSIP code; that is the identifying code that applies to every individual stock or option position. So if I sell CMG, and buy back into TSLA, they would have different

CUSIP identifiers. If I sell an option for $135 strike price, and turn around and replace it with a new position with a $125 strike price, they have different CUSIP identifiers. So pay attention, harvest your tax losses, and if you replace the position, make sure the identifiers are different for 30 days before and after the trade.

If you are in a taxable account, you will start monitoring the gains situation as you get into November and December, and if there are realized gains, you want to look in your portfolio for positions that have unrealized losses. Start to sell those positions to realize the losses, and continue to do this until the net realized total gain for the year is near zero. If you end up with an excess of losses, that is fine too; you can roll that forward indefinitely.

TWO STEPS FORWARD, THEN ONE STEP BACK

You may have experienced this traumatic event in the market already. Everything is going along just peachy. Perhaps the market has been going up for a week or two. Then, wham! Two or three bad down days. Oh, I wish it had just kept going up! That was a lot more fun!

One of the most difficult things to deal with is when you've had this terrible day in the market or a terrible week, and you're depressed over it. I've had this happen to me typically when the markets had a couple of really bad days in a row. It has happened to me probably 10 to 20 times in my career. I start thinking it will never recover.

One thing I've learned in the past four years is that every single time it happened, the event turned out to be shorter-lived than I expected, and not only did it recover, but it went higher.

Every time it did recover, it recovered more quickly than I expected. Sometimes in a week, sometimes in two weeks, sometimes in a month, but it always recovered. And I can honestly say without qualification, every one of those big drops has recovered and been surpassed by greater gains.

In September of 2018, I felt like I was flying high. My portfolio for the year was up YTD by about 70 percent by October of 2018. Then the market started contracting on fear of America's trade war with China, interest rates, and uncertainty in government policy. And by December 31, 2018, I was behind 10 percent in total. I ended up having a rare negative return year!

I wondered if it would ever recover, but it did in the first quarter of 2019 and continued to rise throughout the year. By December 31, 2019, I was up 96 percent for the year!

Here is the mindset you must have to make gains happen after a drop. You're watching the market go down; it's going down, it's going down, you're sitting there dumb-struck, and your portfolio is shrinking. What do you need to do at that time? You must force yourself to nibble in and buy some long-dated calls, either every day or at least every week. What does this do for you? It lets you average in at the bottom of the dip with a leveraged long position, that is long-dated calls two years out. Some of them you'll buy before the market hits its bottom, some of them you'll buy on the day the market did hit its bottom, some of them you'll buy as the market is coming out of the bottom, but you averaged in during the bottom.

It is a problem if the market trades down regularly for two years. We would be very unhappy if we kept buying call options for two years, and the market still hadn't turned around. That would be a real losing situation. So when we talk about dips or contractions, we are talking about doing this in a generally healthy market, and one that is typical of the past several decades when stocks went up.

DO NOT BET THE RANCH

One caveat to all of this is that, ideally, you don't want to put so much of your money into your portfolios, and into your positions, that you're going to lose all your money somehow and have zero, and not be able to start over. I'm not advising you to go broke. You've got to have a little bit of cash available that you have not invested, so that when and if you need to take advantage of a down week or a down month, you've got some dry powder to spend.

The other advantage of keeping a cash cushion is that it will protect you against having a stock put to you some weekend at a discount. As we've discussed, it is not a bad result to buy your favorite stock at a 10 percent discount, but you need sufficient cash on hand to cover the purchase. Remember we discussed that when you sell the put, you will put up cash equal to about 20 percent of what the stock would cost if it were put to you. If that happens, and it is put to you, you will need about 50 percent of what the stock costs, because the margin requirement at most brokerages is 50 percent. It varies by situation, but this is a fairly accurate estimate.

So...keep some cash available to take advantage of opportunities.

KEY POINTS FROM CHAPTER 7

1. Wait until the market, or your favorite stocks, have a big dip, then buy call options at a low price, and hold until they increase in value. Then, roll into the stock at expiration, or sell for a profit.

2. Average in with long-dated calls. Nibble in and buy call options that are two years out on your favorite stocks. Avoid selling puts when the market turns downward to avoid running up a big loss quickly.

3. If you want to be a Sharper Investor, force yourself to nibble in, to average in, maybe not every day, but maybe every third day, or every week, or every two weeks, when the market is declining—even if doing so makes you nervous.

4. Only sell puts on stocks that you want to own, and only buy calls on stocks you want to own. There is a possibility you will end up with these stocks in your portfolio!

5. The only investment that's taxable is a realized gain when the position has been closed out.

6. Keep a cash cushion to protect you from being wiped out, and also to take advantage of big dips.

CONCLUSION

Congratulations! You've now got all the tools you need to start investing.

LET'S REVIEW OUR THREE-POINT FORMULA

There are three points in our formula.

1. Pick the right stocks. In 2020, some of the right stocks were Amazon, Apple, Tesla, Domino's, Chipotle, Facebook, Zoom, Restoration Hardware, Etsy, and a host of others that relate to the stay-at-home strategy. That was 2020. Things change every year.

   Action Alerts PLUS *stock picks are perfectly sufficient to give you some names to work with.*

And, of course, you will pick some yourself, based on the companies you know and love. Disclaimer: I am not in any way receiving compensation for the mention of Action Alerts PLUS.

2. Strategically buy call options two years out at a strike price above the current price, maybe four lines higher priced on the options chart for two-year-out calls. This is to be done when you identify a stock that you think will go up in the next year.

3. Strategically sell put options that are only one or two weeks to expiration, at a strike price roughly 10 percent below the current stock price. This is a different bet for sure. It's still an option of course, but instead of buying a call option two years out, we're going to sell a put option one or two weeks out. This is to be done when you identify a stock that you think will not go down much in the next week or two.

It comes down to your judgment: if you think the
stock has a likelihood of going up in the next year,
you want to buy call options that are two years out.

If you think the stock is not necessarily going
to go up, but you don't think it will go down in the
next week, you want to sell put options that are
one or two weeks out.

And you must limit these trades to your favorite
stocks. You do not want to try this on stocks that you
don't want to own, because when you buy a call option,
there's always the possibility you'll end up owning the
stock at the end, and it should be a stock you'd like to
own. When you sell a put option, there's the possibility
you'll end up owning the stock. So we only sell puts on
our favorite stocks.

WHAT ARE YOU STRIVING FOR?

This is the most exciting part to discuss because you now
have the opportunity to make a huge amount of money,
which will change your life and the life of your family. It
is not unrealistic to expect that you can greatly multiply
your net worth.

The change in my net worth, as a result of following the strategies here, has been pretty amazing. About six years ago I was fortunate to have about $60 million to invest. It was the highest number I had reached in many years of investing. It felt good, but nothing like what happened the next six years. Using these formulas, it grew rapidly and eventually reached $300 million. As you might imagine, that rocked my world, and I felt so good! Admittedly, I am still a long way from reaching my goal of a billion-dollar account, but it is still a huge leap forward. And it was fun and satisfying to do it!

As a result, I know the strategies here work because they worked for me, and can work for you. And it is satisfying on several levels. First, there is the pride of doing it and the knowledge that you did it yourself. That is an incredible accomplishment and will make you feel so good about yourself.

Second, you will be much happier spending money that you made for yourself in the market. Making it yourself is a big difference. The fact that you figured out how to do it, and you did it, is tremendously empowering. It will give you confidence that permeates every aspect of your life.

And another benefit is that you are not turning your money over to some "money manager" who may or may not do a good job for you. My experience is that if a money manager makes a 6 percent a year return, they will try to convince you that it is a good result for you. But it isn't! We are going to work at making 30–50% a year. So you will have control of your own money, and you will have instant liquidity—you can close out a position and get the cash the next day or so if you need it.

Have confidence in yourself that you can do this and achieve excellent portfolio performance. If you doubt your ability to choose the right stocks to start with, then just spend a few hundred dollars and subscribe to *Action Alerts PLUS*. Let them do the research for you! For a few hundred dollars a year, you have your own world-class stock pickers! This is a perfectly sound choice for choosing the right stocks. Look at the list there, and from those stocks, select the ones you like. There are so many that you cannot invest in them all, so cherry-pick the list to narrow it down.

When you have your stock choices picked out, whether you discover them or let this excellent newsletter service do it for you, use the formula we have discussed here. Buy long-dated calls, sell short-dated puts, and watch your portfolio substantially increase!

Remember, if you produce a return annually of 18% or more, you're already beating 99% of the hedge fund managers!

But I think you'll do a lot better than that following the formula here!

I will leave you with one more thought. If you're entirely new to investing, start small and work up to more significant numbers. There's no reason to start big if this is new to you. We all go through a learning process and make mistakes along the way. So make sure you're comfortable with the amount you're putting at risk as you get better at this.

You can find me online in a few different places.

The Sharper Investor: TheSharperInvestor.com
Features Richard's Blog about current stock picks, shows some of his orders and thoughts on favorite stocks and the market.

The Sharper Fund: TheSharperFund.com
Information about Richard's investing philosophy, some past examples, and portfolio performance results.

Richard Thalheimer: RichardThalheimer.com
An overview of Richard's life, the history of The Sharper Image, and press and media appearances.

Richard's Twitter Account: https://twitter.com/ Richard_Solo

Richard Solo: RichardSolo.com
Richard's online hobby store for interesting gadgets for iPhones and iPads.

There you go! We've discussed a lot. You've grasped The Sharper Investor Winning Formula. Now it's time to fly! Make a few trades and see what happens, though I can tell you what is most likely about to happen: you're going to probably double your returns, and start making 30–50% a year! Welcome to the exciting world of investing!

Happy Investing!

Richard

2021 STOCKS I LOVE AND RECOMMEND

The list changes from time to time, and you can see the latest update at my website *TheSharperInvestor.com*. The most important aspect of this section is that you understand how I think about the stocks I know and love. You will have different companies that you have expertise and experience with—I encourage you to create your own master list. Choosing stocks you know and love is one of the key elements of being a Sharper Investor.

CrowdStrike (CRWD)

CrowdStrike is a leading cybersecurity company protecting customers from cyber threats. CrowdStrike's goal, in short, is to stop security breaches before they occur, using cloud-based technologies.

From its inception in 2011, driven by George Kurtz's vision, CrowdStrike was created as a different kind of cybersecurity company. The platform offers a set of cloud-delivered technologies that provides a wide range of products, including antivirus, endpoint detection and response (EDR), device control, managed threat hunting, information technology (IT) hygiene, vulnerability management, and threat intelligence.

Everything I read, and it's a lot, keeps saying that CRWD is the leader in this field, and we know from the news that cybersecurity is a growing threat. CrowdStrike is the one we frequently read about that is well-positioned to offer long-term solutions.

I don't know or use the company. Still, because I read, I recognize what companies are taking the lead in the press, and over time, I've noticed that when companies receive press as an industry leader, the stock usually follows with a price increase.

Tesla (TSLA)

I love Tesla. Elon Musk is a visionary, and Tesla makes an exceptional product. Their first-mover advantage, their software, their vehicle range, and their Supercharger network give them a technological advantage over their competition. Of course, there is competition coming, and time will tell if they maintain their leadership. But I am betting they will. This is a perfect example of a first-mover advantage and market dominance.

Domino's (DPZ)

Domino's Pizza has a system that's far superior to your local pizzeria for ordering and delivery. During the COVID-19 lockdown, Domino's did more business than ever, and lots of new customers became accustomed to using the Domino's app. It is sophisticated, showing you the status of your order cooking and every step in the process—quite interesting to watch. This got them a lot of new followers, and the sales and earnings are really great. It has made for a solid investment.

Amazon (AMZN)

One of the biggest winners of the past few years has been Amazon. Think about this. In 2020, because of the COVID-19 virus, everyone was staying at home. Schools and many businesses were shut down. It was difficult to shop in person, and many items were in short supply. What did you do? You ordered from Amazon and so did all your neighbors. And predictably, Amazon stock soared and continues to soar. The delivery is fast. The Prime delivery is free, for $119 a year, in 2021. The Amazon return privilege is so easy to use. The way they fix their mistakes or defects demonstrates superior customer service. Add all of these variables together, and of course, it's been a fabulous investment.

Amazon is an expensive stock, over $3,200 a share in August 2021. For the average person, that's a big investment to make. But here again, we're not buying stocks outright. We're buying call options two years out on the stock. And the Amazon share that's $3,200, for example, has a long dated call option that's only $380. You control the same number of shares for $380 that you do for $3,200. To me, it's obvious. I'd rather control the same number of shares for $380 than control the same number of shares for $3,200. Admittedly Amazon is still a big investment, because one call contract is for 100 shares, so at $380 each it is a $38,500 investment. Of course, to control 100 shares at $3,200 is a $320,000 investment, or on a 50 percent margin, it is still a $160,000 investment. All of these are big numbers, but the call contract is a better use of your cash.

Apple (AAPL)

Let's talk about Apple products. Like most people, I grew up using Microsoft Windows. Everyone had a Windows computer, right? Probably a Dell. Then somehow, I decided finally to try an Apple computer. And of course, it was a little strange at first. It took a while to get the hang of it. The operating system is different.

I was still at The Sharper Image at the time—this was 2001—as the CEO and founder. And an amazing thing happened. Apple came out with the iPod—a music device, an MP3 player. And I realized this was a game-changer in portable music players. It was so much better than anything else on the market.

Interestingly, The Sharper Image was the only retail store to sell the iPod at first, because Apple didn't have retail stores then. And, the product was flying out of the stores! Every morning a shipment would arrive, and it'd be completely sold out by 11 a.m. So I knew there was a big thing happening here, and I started buying Apple stock.

Nowadays I use Apple computers all the time. I will never ever again touch a Windows computer. In some jobs, you have to, but in my job, I don't have to. I can use whatever I want. And they're just so much better made; they're much better quality in terms of design and the operating system. And, I have repeatedly bought other Apple products, like the iPhone, the iPad, and the Apple Watch. They are all exceptional. And as a result, Apple has been a fabulous investment.

Chipotle (CMG)

Chipotle was able to make major moves in the past five years to improve the quality of their business in terms of food safety, cleanliness, digital ordering, drive-through lanes, and new menu items. They also brought in a superb choice for CEO in Brian Niccol. He had previously done very well at Taco Bell, and when he moved to Chipotle, he injected a healthy dose of digital marketing, menu changes, and a rigorous management shake-up to get rid of the problems of the past.

The net result is that Chipotle has been on a tear ever since Niccol joined, and the stock has marched steadily upwards.

SalesForce Management (CRM)

Of all the quarterly results I listen to, none have been more consistently upbeat than listening to Marc Benioff at CRM. He just keeps delivering beat after beat, and that's the result that investors want to see.

I have a lot of confidence in CRM, and continue to sell puts and buy calls on every dip.

Facebook (FB)

Facebook is obviously a powerhouse in social media, and Mark Zuckerberg is a brilliant creator and strategist. They have done so well in most every area they have reached, and acquiring Instagram is an example of their smart moves. My thinking is that Facebook will continue to be the dominant player in social media—another example of the advantage of first-mover and market dominance.

Alphabet (GOOG)

Along with Apple, this is one of my favorite tech plays. Over the years Google has proved to be a dominant force.

Advertising of course is their forte, but buying YouTube was shrewd also. And they have fingers in many new technologies, including self-driving cars and AI. They will continue to be a major player for years to come.

Nvidia (NVDA)

Every product area seems to require more computer chips today, including video games of course, but also cars and many other products. There are several chip players, but my favorite is Nvidia. The founder and CEO, Jensen Huang, is brilliant, and Nvidia is in many areas that will be important in the future. In an August 2021 earnings release, Huang said, "Nvidia's pioneering work in accelerated computing continues to advance graphics, scientific computing and AI."

In that earnings release, NVDA outperformed in every metric, and I feel confident it will continue to do well and see future appreciation in its stock price.

Align Technology, Inc. (ALGN)

When my 13-year-old daughter (at the time) needed braces for her teeth, we went to an orthodontist. The first orthodontist we consulted told us, "Oh, you've got to use metal braces. Invisalign wouldn't work for this situation."

Invisalign is a medical-grade plastic retainer that you put in your mouth, and it is virtually invisible. It's not permanent. You can pop it in and out anytime. It's a replacement for conventional metal braces and much easier to use. There are no metal brackets or wires to detract from your smile while undergoing treatment. You just push it in your mouth and wear it, whereas metal braces, of course, have to be fitted, and tweaked, and tightened, and it's a big pain. With the Invisalign system, the computer photos are used to create a bunch of progressive retainers, and you use the first one for two weeks, then progress to the second, and so on until all the retainers are used.

The other orthodontist that we like a lot said, "Invisalign would work fine." There was no reason to use metal braces. So I'm thinking, I wonder if Align is a good investment?

Then, a week or so later, I happened to be at an event reception, and I struck up a conversation with some guy I didn't know. He turned out to be a 70-year-old orthodontist who was still practicing. I asked him about Invisalign. He says, "Oh, yes. That's definitely taking over the market. No one is going to be using metal braces in ten years."

I'm thinking, How fascinating is this? Here's a guy with a lot of experience, 70 years old, telling me that he even thinks Invisalign is taking over the market.

This stock has done great for me. It's been one of my best investments over the years. I own a lot of it, and it's all unrealized gains because I continue to believe they're the market leader, despite some competition that has not hurt them. I expect they'll continue to be the market leader in the future. Here again, the critical point is we want to let our unrealized gains ride—we want to let them go on. We don't want to cash out as long as we have confidence in the company, and still like the strategy, and believe in what they're doing.

Taser (AXON)

In Chapter 3, I discussed their position as a market leader. Still, I also like their mission statement: "Axon is dedicated to making the bullet obsolete, reducing social conflict, ensuring criminal justice systems are fair and effective and building for racial diversity, equity, and inclusion. We are working with law enforcement and community leaders across the nation on the changes needed. Axon is here for a change."

"Axon is proud to be a change agent, particularly at a time when our customers, partners, and communities are facing global challenges around reimagining justice and policing," says Axon CEO and Founder Rick Smith. "The goal is to bring law enforcement and communities together to solve some of the biggest problems facing our citizens, police departments, and government."

What's the moral of the story? I learned about this company by researching the product and the company.

I noticed that it's the market leader, and I believe that police cameras are an important tool for the future. Nibble into the long-dated call options, or sell conservatively priced puts every week.

CarParts (PRTS)

I've been using CarParts for a couple of months. Every time I order, I'm pleasantly surprised at how reasonable the price of the part is. I'm also impressed with how quickly they deliver. I'm thoroughly impressed with the quality of their website. It's an excellent system. Let me recommend it to you. If you need a car part, go to *CarParts.com*.

About six months later, by accident, I see the CEO on CNBC talking about their business, and I realize this is a publicly-traded company. I start nibbling into long-dated call options on PRTS because I'm satisfied with my experience with the company. I've used it, I like it, and I like the CNBC interview that the CEO did.

Intuitive Surgical (ISRG)

Intuitive Surgical makes surgical products under the brand name da Vinci that allows the surgeon to sit in his hospital or his office and work controls, like a video game. And at the other end is a robot that's doing the actual cutting and stitching on a human patient. And because the robot has more delicate fingers than any human and because the robot is more steady, it can operate surgically, remotely, and do a better job than doing it in person.

The actual surgeon might be in the room next door, or more amazingly to me, they could be doing it across the world. A surgeon in New York could be operating on someone in Africa because the technique is exactly the same. You move the levers in the surgeon's office, and the robot does the surgery at the other end. There might be nurses or doctors of course, in attendance. But how fascinating; this is the way the world is going, and the market leader is Intuitive Surgical.

Restoration Hardware—now RH (RH)

I'm really impressed with RH and the quality of their furniture. I'm impressed with Gary Friedman, the CEO—his interviews are so good.

Most public companies have a quarterly open earnings call with questions and answers where you can often hear the CEO talk to the analysts. In this case, you can hear Gary Friedman talking to analysts with their questions. I'm listening to this discussion, and I am also buying their furniture, and have used their return privilege, and have been impressed with the quality of the construction and the fabrics; in summary, it is a really positive experience all the way through. I am so impressed. Everything checks out and looks good. And to add more convincing evidence, it comes out in the news that Gary Friedman, the CEO, has a tremendous compensation package that includes a lot of stock options if the stock hits a certain level.

In this package, the stock has to go to a certain level above where it is now; it's got to stay there, and if it does, Gary Friedman makes literally hundreds of millions of dollars. My thought is that I have followed this guy's career, and he's been very successful for a long time. He's very ambitious. He's still in his prime, and he's got this compensation package that is going to pay him hundreds of millions of dollars if RH does well. He's got a strategy that's bold and audacious and is proving itself to be very successful. This is a great combination of factors coming together, and so far it has really been a winner for the company and the stock price.

25 PRO TRADING TIPS FOR YOU TO USE

1. Understand How and When To Use a Limit Order.

Limit orders ensure that you do not pay more than you want because you enter the "limit" of the price you want to pay. Most of us are familiar with market orders, which gives you a price that is usually somewhere between the bid and the asked price. That is fine, but sometimes you want to be pickier and get a slightly better price.

Let's consider the example where you are buying a long-dated call option. The bid is $20, and the ask is $21. You might enter a limit order of $20.50, meaning you will pay up to that, but no more than $20.50. Then, you select the time for the order to be valid, and I usually select "60 days" because if it doesn't fill that day, maybe it will fill tomorrow or the next day. There isn't any particular rush since the call option has a two-year life. After entering the order, you check the order status, and you'll see if it is filled or not. If not, you can just leave it and wait for it to fill in an hour or a day.

If you want it to fill now, and if it has not, that means no one is accepting your price. To make it fill, you need to raise your offer a bit. You can click on "change order" and put in a higher bid, perhaps $20.60. Then you enter this new bid and check the order status again. Eventually, the order will fill, and if not, you can raise your limit to $20.65. So that is how a limit order works, to make sure you do not overpay.

One of the best uses of limit orders is to sell a position that you'd like to close out. The idea is that you put in a limit order for a higher price, good for 60 days. Then you can relax and forget about it for the moment. What you are hoping is that the stock price will pop up momentarily, and your order will fill.

This is one of the very best ways to initiate a new position. Put in a slightly low limit offer to buy, and sit back and wait. It might fill today, tomorrow, or next week. This works especially well buying a two-year-out call option. Since it doesn't expire for two years, you should not really care if your new call option order fills today, tomorrow, or next week. You have two years until expiration. So put in your low limit order, click "good for 60 days," and let it fill on its own time. There is no rush, and you will get a good price.

If you want to own the actual stock, you might sell a put option instead, again using a limit order to get a really good price. Only two things can happen: you'll end up keeping the premium, or you'll end up owning the stock at a substantial discount.

2. Nibble In, Average In, or Leg In— Just Don't Take Big Bites

One of the best techniques you can use is to average in when you want to establish a new position. Let's imagine that you want to put $10,000 into a new position. Rather than buying $10,000 of the stock or call option, only buy $2,500 of it. Then wait a few days, or a week, or longer. After that period of time, you buy another $2,500 of it. Then wait another few days, week, or two weeks, or longer, and buy $2,500 again. Finally, after yet another week, or two weeks, or longer, you put in the last $2,500.

What have you accomplished? Well, if the stock has dropped some after the first purchase, you will be happy you are buying more at a lower price. If it continues to drop after your second purchase, you will be even more happy that you waited to buy the third lot. So averaging in helps you to get the best prices.

What if the stock goes up after your first purchase? Obviously, you might wish that you had put the entire $10,000 in to begin, but that is not something that is easy to predict. But at least you did not lose any money. Most experts prefer that you average in to protect yourself against a drop.

3. Harvest Tax Losses and Use Them to Offset Future Gains

If you are in a taxable account, the tax harvest and swap is a great tool for you to use. You look through your portfolio, and you find a position that has a loss. You sell the losing position, and then take the proceeds and invest it into something different. This lets you "harvest" the tax loss, and use it to offset future gains. And, if your losses are larger than your capital gains, you can use the remaining losses to offset up to $3,000 of ordinary taxable income (for married couples filing separately, the limit is $1,500). You can carry leftover losses forward forever. By putting the proceeds to work in another position, you effectively keep yourself in the market, just as before, with an equal chance the position will go up in value.

This is much better than just holding the losing position, because you still have the opportunity for your investment to go up, but you also have banked a tax loss, and that is a valuable tool to offset gains.

The only thing you must do to make this work is to make sure the second stock pick is just as good a pick as the stock you just sold. For example, you sell Apple and buy Google. Or sell Nvidia, and buy AMD. Or sell Chipotle, and buy RH.

Now with call options, this is even easier, and super simple, because if you like the name, you can keep the name. Here is how: you sell your January 2023 call option and book the loss, and turn around and buy the same stock call option, but change the strike price. For example, buy the same month, January 2023, but at a strike price that is $10 lower. That will qualify as a different stock, which seems odd since it is practically the same, but since they have different CUSIP numbers, they will act as different stock positions for IRS purposes. To be super safe with this strategy, I suggest switching the month. For example, if you close out the January 2023 strike price of $350, turn around and start a new position of December 2022 strike price of $340. That is definitely different.

4. Roll Your Losing Call Option To Get the Tax Loss

Similar to the tax harvesting above, anytime you have a call option that is in the red, think about closing it out, and buy the same position back, but with a one-month earlier expiration date. You have harvested the tax loss, and you still have essentially the same position. If you like it, you still have it, but you have banked the tax loss.

The IRS will allow this, and not consider it a wash sale, because each option has a unique CUSIP number, and that is what is determinative for tax purposes.

5. Friday Afternoon Dips Are Buying Opportunities

This is more anecdotal since I have not researched the statistics. In my experience, it is not uncommon for markets to drop on a Friday afternoon as the market approaches the close. This seems especially true on three-day weekends. The reason is that big funds and big traders do not want to hold stocks over the weekend and be exposed to the unknown of what events may happen over the weekend.

That presents an opportunity for you to make an opportunistic purchase late Friday afternoon. It might also affect your put option position. Many times I am holding a put option position that has been in the money all week, and then late Friday afternoon the stock price swoons and the stock ends up getting put to me on Saturday. I usually do not cover the position late Friday afternoon and take the loss, because I have confidence that when Monday comes, the stock will probably bounce back some. I can't tell you how many times this has happened. I was ahead all week, it swoons on Friday, the stock is put to me and I'm showing a slight loss, but after the market opens Monday, I will have a slight gain. A slightly different version of taking advantage of this is to sell a put option on Friday afternoon, for the following Friday's expiration. You're just taking advantage of the Friday swoon.

6. Never Place Too Big a Bet On One Stock, Even When You're Confident

I can't tell you how many times I see a chance to make money on what I think is a sure thing. This has happened a lot with a put option expiring in a week or two. I'm so sure that my instincts are correct, and I want to make a killing. So, I place a large bet. I'm really confident, so then I double the bet. So it is definitely a big investment. And what happens? Friday expiration comes, and surprise, the stock has dropped a lot, and my winning sure bet has, in reality, turned into a big loser! This has happened more than once.

What did I learn from this? Don't get overconfident, and don't put too much money into one position. Of course, you can bet big now and then, but don't make it such an outsized position that you can get really burned if it doesn't turn out the way you expected.

7. Diversify Your Choices, But Not Too Much

Warren Buffet famously said that he is against diversification. "Diversification is a protection against ignorance," Buffett once said. "[It] makes very little sense for those who know what they're doing."

In other words, if you are completely diversified, you have not really made any choice at all. Instead, you have chosen to let the market be your guide. And that is not necessarily a bad thing, but it will not let you beat the averages because you are now just tracking the averages. If you want to beat the averages, you must find individual stocks that will outperform.

To balance the discussion, my point of view is that, as Buffet points out, you must pick individual stocks that beat the averages. However, within that group of stocks, I recommend some diversification, meaning different sectors. I have Tesla, Chipotle, Amazon, Salesforce and Apple, which are somewhat diversified, though still very different from the major averages.

8. Dips Are Buying Opportunities
If Earnings and Revenues Are Up

This is a common occurrence; you see it occasionally that a company has a really good report, and yet the stock sinks the next day. It doesn't seem to make sense. Wouldn't you expect the stock to go up in that situation?

Especially if they not only beat on earnings, beat on revenue, and also give an upbeat outlook for the future?

What has happened is that the analyst community has gotten ahead of itself, and expectations were too high. Even though the company did really well, the stock was already priced to expect perfection, and sometimes a rosy outlook is not "perfect" enough, and so the stock sinks some.

A real life example of this happened on April 27, 2021 with Tesla. The earnings report released on April 26 was excellent. I don't know that it could have been better than what it was. Nevertheless, the next day the stock dropped $30 or 4 percent to $708. This did not make sense...the report was excellent, but sometimes you see these "sell on the news" moments.

For me, if I believe in the company's long-term strategy, and the current excellent earnings report and outlook seem strongly positive, I take this situation as an opportunity to add to my long position. I know the company is going to do well and this is just a momentary blip. I have some long-dated call options, and now I take advantage and buy some more.

Don't be discouraged when this scenario happens, but rather look at it as a dip that invites you to get in.

9. Distinguish Between Momentary
Events and Real Changes

Similarly to the drop in earnings, it is not uncommon that a stock sells off on a momentary event, but you correctly analyze that the strategy and performance have not changed; it is just a momentary event of no real consequence. This used to happen in 2016 when Chipotle was having some problems with foodborne illnesses in their restaurants. They did get the problems under control, but even a year later, if someone reported a food illness on a chat board, it would get picked up by the news, and the stock would react the next day. In other words, investors were concerned that the food problems had resurfaced. That was not the case, but people were jittery anyway. These isolated incidents got blown out of proportion. It was not real change; it was just a momentary event that did nothing to change the strategy or performance.

This happened in the last week of June 2021, when Boeing had unexpected news. A 25-year-old 737 had an engine failure, and ditched into the ocean off Honolulu. The headline that day was that the stock slid (2 percent) as a result. However, this strikes me as a momentary event, not any real news that will change the trajectory of the stock upward.

Another example of this happens occasionally with Tesla. Maybe a car catches fire, or a battery explodes. Is that a real change? No it isn't, as Tesla explains, there are a lot of fires in gas fuel cars too—in fact many more than in Teslas. But the stock reacts because investors cannot tell the difference between real change and a momentary event. This presents a buying opportunity.

10. Take Advantage of Good Stocks Sinking on Down Days

There are various reasons why good stocks are dragged down on a sinking market day. Some traders need to cash in their good stocks so that they have adequate liquidity to cover losses on their bad positions.

Another reason is that a lot of funds are computer-driven, and when the computer sees the market going down, it puts in sell orders. However, the computer probably cannot decide which stocks to hold on to, and which stocks to sell. It just sells because it can tell things are heading down.

Many times I have seen this happen! The stock market sinks for some reason, because interest rates are climbing on a particular day. So what happens? All the stocks go down, including Domino's Pizza and Google.

This also seems to happen every time interest rates tick up. But what does a small increase in ten-year interest rates have to do with people ordering pizza, or searching on Google? Clearly there is no correlation! But all these stocks are in baskets held by large funds, and when the market has a knee-jerk reaction to an interest rate rise, all the stocks in the basket are traded lower. You can take advantage of this.

Use this opportunity to average into a new long position. It will probably be a winner, because the reason for the discount is not a good reason, it is just the way the market reacts, and has nothing to do with the value of the company. There is good reason to expect the stock will come back up.

11. Don't Sell Puts in Earnings Week

Selling put options one week out can be a good formula for making some easy profits. I personally sell puts every week, betting that a good stock will not drop too much by Friday, and if it does, that might be a way to pick up that stock at a 10–15% discount. Why not? It is on sale, and I love a sale.

However, one thing I've learned is this is a risky strategy the week that the earnings are being reported. The stock will perhaps have a big move one way or the other, and my general rule is to avoid selling puts that expire in a week, if earnings are being reported that week. I figure better safe than sorry since it is difficult to predict how the stock will behave when the earnings come out.

12. When Markets Are Plummeting,
Resist the Urge To Do Anything

When the markets are plummeting, don't do anything. There are times when the market is plummeting because of some news, or perceived change in the economic situation. What should you do on a day when the market is dropping precipitously? My advice is to just sit tight; you don't want to sell just because your stocks have dropped suddenly. And you don't want to buy if the market is dropping precipitously, because it may continue. So what you need to do is just sit tight. I wait. Generally, this will be a good course of action.

My experience over many years is that you will be pleased if you just sit and wait for a day or two or three. These dramatic drops often revert to the mean more quickly than you would think. So just stay calm and watch.

13. Thinking of Selling a Losing Position?
Only Sell Half Unless You Have Conviction

This is a common situation. You have a position, you are behind—that is, in the red—and you are thinking of selling out. Should you? If you're not certain what you want to do, just average out. Sell half now, and wait a bit.

If it turns around, you will be pleased you didn't sell it all. And if it continues down, you will be happy you already got rid of half of it, and now you can sell the rest. If half is too big a chunk for you to want to sell, then do it 25 percent at a time, and get out of it in four equal transactions.

However, if you are behind in the position and the stock is not particularly meaningful to you, then I would sell the entire position and get the tax loss—sell it all, and be done with looking at it. This is especially true in a taxable account because you book the loss and can put the money into another stock that has an equal chance of going up.

14. Ahead in a Position—Double Or More... And Cannot Decide Whether To Cash Out? *Sell Half and Let the Other Half Ride*

Jim Cramer often mentions this situation, especially when you have doubled your money from where you started. He advises to sell half, take the profit, and as he likes to say, "Now you are playing with the house's money." For me personally, I usually do not sell half. Rather, I hang on to all of it if the story still seems sound, and the company's strategy resonates with me; that's because I am in a taxable account and live in California. The income tax would take about 40 percent or more of the gain, and I often have some very big percentage gains. So I tend to let my winners keep going. But if you are in a non-taxable account, your situation allows you to cash out some.

> > **184** < <

15. If You're in a Position that Is Losing, or You Want Out, Place a Standing Limit Order

We often forget to put in a limit order to get out. But you should have a limit order in place, good for 60 days. The stock may have a strong move one day and hit your limit order, and get executed. You can't watch the market every second of every day, so let the limit order stand guard and watch out for you.

16. Only Close Positions Out at the Bottom for the Purpose of a Tax Loss

One of the worst mistakes you can make, in my opinion, is to get worried when your position has dropped a lot and decide to sell out at the bottom. The normal human emotion tells you to get out after a bruising week, but my experience tells me there will be a better opportunity in the future to get out.

We definitely do not want to be the investor that buys high and sells low, but that is what you are doing if you get discouraged and cash out at the bottom. Just sit tight and do not do anything! Wait, and things will probably get better. And if you cannot control the desire to sell some, then just sell 25 percent or 50 percent, and wait for things to brighten up.

If you can use the tax loss to offset other gains in a taxable account, that is a different situation.

I would take the full loss and put the money to use in another position that has an equally good chance of going up. That way you get the best of both: you have the tax loss booked, and you are still in a stock that you think will go up.

17. Do Not Initiate a New Long Position at the New 52-Week High Price

It seems that a normal human emotion is to want to get into a new long position when the market is hitting new highs. It just seems like it is going up, up, and up, and we want to get in. However, my experience tells me that there will probably be a lower entry point in the future, and getting in at the new high is probably not going to turn out well. There are always dips, and you should wait for one.

You should average in, and you could use limit orders to get the best price. The worst that can happen is that it continues to go up in price, and you missed getting in some. The best that can happen is that you continue to average in, and you get some at a lower price. Either outcome is a good result in my opinion.

18. Use Margin Sparingly but Wisely

Beginning investors are advised to steer clear of using margin, because it allows you to double your upside, or double your downside as well, and that can be dangerous to your portfolio if it goes bad.

For me personally, it has been an excellent technique to boost my returns. I am borrowing at a low interest rate, 2% or less, and I am earning 30 to 100% a year on the borrowed money! So it is great when it works. The catch here is that it must work, that is, the investments need to go up.

That is a judgment call that only you can make for yourself, though I think a margin is a valuable tool. Just don't overdo it at the beginning. Get your toe in the water, try some margin, and see if it is working for you.

19. Want To Go Short on a Stock?
Buy Put Options Instead

There are times when you want to bet that a stock will go down because you don't believe in the company or its strategy. However, for the retail investor, it is very difficult to short a stock. You may have tried it, and found out that the stock is not available to short. And, there is often a high carrying cost to borrow and short a stock.

What to do? Here is a much simpler approach. Buy a put option on the stock, and choose an expiration date that is long-dated, at least a year out for the expiration or even two years out. Buying a put is in effect a synthetic short, but much easier to do because it is readily available and requires you to put up less of your own money. Just look at the options available, choose a put that is out in the future, and choose a strike price that is about 10 percent lower than the current market price for the stock. Then just sit back and wait for your strategy to take hold!

20. In Taxable Accounts, Avoid Wash Sales. Look Backward and Forward 30 Days to Identify Wash Transactions

This is a complicated subject, known by the IRS as the wash sale rule. Basically, in a taxable account, it disallows you to use the loss that you take on the stock sale if you buy the stock back within 30 days of the sale. What is confusing is that the rule applies to transactions 30 days after, or 30 days before, the loss sale.

What to do? Well, if you get rid of the wash stock position altogether so that there is none of the offending stock left in your portfolio, then you have solved your problem. You can now take the loss.

There is one other way that you can sell the stock for a loss, and buy it back right away, and avoid running afoul of the rule. And that is to buy back a call option on the stock, rather than buying the actual stock. A call option on the same stock is not treated as the same stock for the purpose of this rule. And as we've discussed, options with different strike prices or different expiration dates are not treated as wash sales, because they have different CUSIP numbers.

21. Your Total Number of Positions Must Equal the Total You Can Actually Watch

Limit your portfolio to 10, or maximum 20, different stock positions. Options on the same stock can be treated as one stock for this purpose.

Jim Cramer advises you to limit it to 10 stocks (or call options) because he thinks that keeping track of 10 companies is enough work for the average investor. I think it is perfectly fine to have 20 different companies, or even 25, though admittedly it is a bit more work to follow them all.

Once you get more than 25 different companies in your portfolio, it is challenging to follow them all, though for more experienced investors it should not be a problem.

22. Make Extra Cash Each Week by Selling Covered Calls

Selling covered calls on the stock you own is an easy way to make extra profits. Say you own Tesla at $700. You sell call options for the exact number of shares that you own, with a strike price perhaps of $720, and you collect a premium of perhaps $500 for the week for selling this call option expiring in two weeks.

If the stock does not reach $720 by the expiration date, then you keep the $500 as a short-term gain. If the stock is above $720 on expiration, then you must sell your shares for $720.

That might be a good result, though if the stock shot to $750 you would be unhappy you sold out at $720. If the stock only gets to $709 or has sunk below $700 at expiration, you are delighted to have gotten the $500 call option premium.

There are tax considerations to take into account with this strategy. If you have very little gain in the stock position, you don't mind having the stock called away from you. However, if you have a big gain in the stock, you do not want to have it sold and then trigger a big realized gain tax bill.

A lot of my stock positions do have very large percentage gains in them, so I rarely sell covered calls. But it can be very profitable if you are in a tax-free account to sell covered calls every week.

23. Only Add to a Long Position
If You Can Do It At a Better Price
Than You Paid Before

Often, you have a position that you like, and you would like to add to the position. Perhaps you own a long-dated call option and you want to add more. Or perhaps you own a stock and want to add more to it. One good rule to follow is to only add to the position if you can buy more at a lower price than your average price paid. That way, you are averaging down in cost.

And conversely, if you would be adding to the position at a higher price than your average cost, then you generally do not want to buy more.

Adding to an existing position at a lower cost will ensure you keep averaging down your cost, and will help you avoid paying too much. There are of course exceptions to this rule if you love the stock and feel confident it is going higher, but this is a good general rule to follow.

24. Force Yourself to Buy into a Declining Market

This is one of the most emotionally difficult things to do. You want to take advantage of a dip in the market by buying long-dated call options. The reason it is difficult is that when the market is falling, it is hard to press the "buy" button! There is a good chance it will be even lower tomorrow.

Jim Cramer says it this way: "We've seen this happen countless times, people, yet it's very hard for people to remember that you're supposed to buy, not sell, when stocks are collapsing."

The way to handle this is to do it in small increments. Buy a tiny position, wait a day or two or three, and buy a bit more. Average your investment into the decline. You have an excellent chance of buying some before the bottom, buying some at the bottom, and buying some after the bottom.

Remember, no one can pick the bottom, not even the best traders. But you can average in around the bottom, and that is a winning strategy!

25. Hold Onto Your Best Stock Gains
Forever...Unless This Happens

If you have a big position with large gains, let it ride. Do not give in to the temptation to sell for a quick profit. Sure, it feels good to book a profit, and it's been said "you can't go broke taking a profit." I agree with that, but it has also been said that the "best holding period is forever." When you hold on, you do not pay any income tax, which is a big point in a taxable account.

Sure, there will be the inevitable dips along the way, but why not just stay the course? Consider this: if you had put $5,000 into Walmart stock in October 1970, and held on, and never sold a share, today you would have more than $74 million dollars! That is incredible, and you would have been very tempted to sell along the way, right? There were certainly dips in price along the way, and you might have thought you should get out while you still had some profit remaining. But the best thing you could have done was just sit tight and hold on!

Oh, there is a big "but" if this happens: you think the company is heading for problems, such as increased competition, poor marketing strategy, or whatever could bring it down. In that case, you should sell and get out. You could be wrong, and it could turn out to be the next Walmart, but that is the risk you take.

You do not want to hang on to a stock once you have decided it is going down. You want to get out. Unless it's Walmart!

ABOUT
THE AUTHOR

Richard Thalheimer led The Sharper Image to its peak as CEO with annual revenues of $750 million, 200 stores, catalogs, an online store, and 4,000 employees. The company became a public corporation in 1987 when its stock was listed on Nasdaq. He chronicled his journey as an entrepreneur in his first book, *Sharper Image Success*, which was named #1 Best Seller in five categories on Amazon at launch. (He recommends the audiobook, which he reads himself!)

Richard Thalheimer's legacy to business, retail, and humanity is substantial and pervasive. In many ways, he revolutionized the way we think, live, and play. His enthusiasm and successful entrepreneurship brought a new level of quality and innovation to the consumer experience. He single-handedly created the upscale gadget market sector.

Thalheimer now runs The Sharper Fund, a successful private fund. He is a stock guru and investing expert, concentrating in the area of consumer products, companies, and market movements. His experience talking to analysts for 20 years as the CEO of The Sharper Image has given him great insight into how Wall Street analysts think, and consequently, when and why investors should confidently follow their judgments.

He communicates with his audience with his blog: *TheSharperInvestor.com*. Richard has taken what he has learned through decades of investing and made it accessible to investors via the web. He offers investing wisdom, stock picks, and specific trading examples that inspire the first-time investor and the seasoned investor. His goal is to empower investors to skillfully trade options independently by reducing risk and maximizing long-term gain.

For more information about Richard's career, visit *RichardThalheimer.com*.

Made in the USA
Las Vegas, NV
14 June 2022

50247739R00136